I0181904

BETWEEN THE SHEETS:

God's design for SEX ...

BETWEEN THE SHEETS:

God's design for SEX ...

Pastor J.O. Burns, Sr.

VISION 300 PUBLISHING

Copyright ©2013, by Vision 300 Publishing

All rights reserved. No part of this book may be produced, scanned, or distributed in any printed or electronic form without written permission. Please do not participate in or encourage piracy of copyrighted materials in violation of the author's rights. Purchase only authorized editions.

Manufactured in the United States of America.

This publication is designed to provide accurate and authoritative information in regard to the subject matter covered. It is sold with the understanding that the publisher is not engaged in rendering legal, medical, psychological, psychiatric or other professional services. If you require this or any other expert assistance, you should seek services of a competent professional.

ISBN 978 – 1 – 62590 – 121 - 7

Visit:
www.thewordcentercogic.com
www.twcvision300.org

Photographer: Sadie Lynn's Photography
Book Cover Design: Kori Joseph Hill

DEDICATION
and
ACKNOWLEDGMENTS

This book is dedicated in loving memory of my late grandmother, First Lady Wilhelmina Burns and to my wonderful mother, Esther Pullings. To my family: my lovely wife, Nicole; my daughter, Sacha; my son Jeffery Burns II; and my granddaughter, Ayana. This book is also dedicated to all those who seek to do the will of the Lord and will use the book to tear down enemy strongholds.

I would like to thank Minister Kourtney Bri-onne King and Pastor Terell Ward for their input and the hours spent collaborating with me on this book. I would also like to thank Evangelist Connie White for her help in editing the manuscript.

Special thanks go to the J.O. Burns Ministries Team, the pastors and member churches of Vision 300, those that attended the *Between the Sheets Conferences* and attended the round table discussions for this book. I also want to thank the bishops, preachers and teachers that have been instrumental in speaking into my life.

Table of Contents

INTRODUCTION

For twelve years, the Lord has prompted me to write this book. Part of my destiny and purpose in God is to tear down Satan's strongholds of lust and sexual addiction and to impart healing to the wounded through the knowledge of God's design for sex. Sexual addiction festers in the Body of Christ because the Church tends to hide it instead of attacking it head on with the knowledge of how it affects our spiritual walk and our relationship with God. We are overstuffed with sexual images in mass media, taught wrong information in our schools and given no information in our churches to conquer Satan's greatest strategy, which is to use our flesh against us.

God has called me to empower individuals with divine knowledge and understanding of His Will and His design for sex, and to help Christians to uncover their spiritual weapons, in Christ, necessary to pull down the strongholds of sexual addiction. God wants the Body of Christ to be free and to flow in His Will.

My Testimony

I grew up in a dysfunctional environment. I was a preacher's kid (fourth generation in the Church of God in Christ) who witnessed many anointed men and women in the gospel brought down by sexual addictions. For as long as I can remember, the enemy has used lust and sexual addiction to thwart my ministry and to cripple my walk. Satan is a thief who comes only to kill and steal and destroy.[1] For many years, Satan has tried to use what God meant for good — my sexuality — to hinder my destiny in God. I remember that at four years of age two teenage girls touched me inappropriately. I ran when they let me go, however, this was the beginning of many years battling sexual addictions.

The incident with the teenage girls affected the way I grew into puberty and how I viewed sex as an adolescent and young adult. That incident opened a door to sexual perversion. When sexual perversion enters a life at an early age, it brings sexual excitement and sexual curiosity too

---

[1] John 10:10

1

early in life. According to God's design, sexual exploration is reserved for a later time. The incident at the age of four opened a door of sexual exploration where even in the first grade I remember bringing pretzels to a girl at school to entice her to go behind the piano and to pull her panties down and show me her vagina. I can recite many stories about how, at a very young age, I was exploring sexual perversion. Too early in life, the enemy was shaping my view of sex to be one of illicit sex outside God's design, and he was setting me up to fail.

At the age of thirteen, I began to play with myself and had my first orgasm through masturbation. From then and until I was thirty-eight years of age, I was in bondage to masturbation. At the age of seventeen, I lost my virginity and began to sleep with many women. From the age of seventeen to nineteen, I had over four hundred female sexual partners. The incident with the two teenage girls at the age of four started a life of bondage, but by the power of the Holy Spirit sexual addiction has been broken in my life.

Today, I testify that at the age of thirty-eight I was delivered from an addiction to masturbation. I was married to my beautiful wife, Nicole, and we suffered many problems sexually because I preferred my hand over her. I recall traveling to Sweden alone and being propositioned by a young lady. I did not acknowledge or accept her proposition, but fled to my hotel room. However, in my hotel room, as I was about to masturbate, I cried out to the Lord: "Lord, no more! No more! I want this broken." From that day to this I have never again masturbated. Being freed from an addiction to masturbation has improved sex in my marriage. I now experience more enjoyable sex with my Wife and I perform better as a lover.

This book is testimony to my battle with sexual addictions and what God taught me in the battle. It is also a road map to deliverance. The Christian faith has taken the wounds in Jesus' hands and combined them with the Word of God in Job 5:18, and come up with a saying that "wounded hands heal best." I believe that my battle with sexual addictions can help many be delivered from the same. My ministry is a testimony to that very deliverance. Many have been delivered from sexual addictions as they listen to the Word of God preached in my ministry and gain knowledge and understanding of God's design for sex. In addition, when a Believer studies on a particular subject — especially to deal with bondage in their own life — the result is increased wisdom, knowledge and understanding about how to overcome in that area of sin. God gives wisdom not only for the individual fight but also wants that Believer to share with others the knowledge and understanding gained.

Images of Illicit SEX Are Everywhere

According to a report by David Satcher, M.D., Ph.d. Former U.S. Surgeon General, "More than one half of the programming on television has sexual content". As you are exposed to these television images, and exposed to the images and words spoken in music videos, demonic activity picks up to distract and discourage you from releasing the strongholds of sexual addictions. You can expect to be attacked as Satan uses your flesh against you!! The enemy wants to kill your faith by putting you in condemnation and having you think that you will never be free from sexual addictions. Satan is trying to steal your joy and discourage you from advancing in the Kingdom of God.

I'm not trying to scare you. I just want you aware of the strategies of your enemy. Satan always attacks the areas where we are weakest. So, be prayerful as you read this book and, by faith, allow the Holy Spirit to minister to you to break strongholds of sexual addictions in your life. If you have a godly spouse, the two of you should be praying together as you read this book because the information contained herein is the very thing the enemy wants to keep away from you. Satan wants you to stay in bondage and he will come against your marriage and every area of your life to keep you there. In fact, *I bind the hand of the enemy right now and declare deliverance over you, in Jesus' name. Amen.*

The open and direct way I approach sex and sexually perverse acts may shock you because most of the topics discussed in this book are not spoken about in Church. The Church must face the reality that sexual addictions are destroying our society and keeping Christians from a life of total victory. I have been in Church all of my life and I've seen the leaders dance around most discussions about sex or speak in generalities. We need God's Word to shine a spot light on sexual perversion in order to have deliverance in the area of sexual addictions. The Word of God is our guide for life and there is no problem for which God's Word does not have a solution.

As you read, remember that everything in the Bible is true — it is Sprit breathed and for your benefit. Satan is a liar and the author of lies!![2] Because of his consistent ministry of lies, we often base our lives on his word instead of the Word of God. In order to be free and walking in the abundance that Jesus died to give us, you must be relentless and persistent in trusting God's ability and His desire to have you free and living a healthy, abundant life. In John 10:10, Jesus announced His purpose in coming to die on the cross: *"I came that they may have life, and have it abundantly."*[3] God is faithful to accomplish His Word in your life if you trust Him and fight the good fight of faith. Without faith you cannot please God and neither will you be a threat to Satan and his forces.

Throughout this book, I reference God's Word to bring out the principles that you should meditate and internalize. (All scriptures are from the NIV unless otherwise noted.) Remember that *"All Scripture is God-breathed and is useful for teaching, rebuking, correcting and training in righteousness, so that the servant of God may be thoroughly equipped for every good work."*[4] Please study and meditate on the scriptures referenced so that your mind will be renewed by the Godly wisdom and principles found in those scriptures.

If I touch on something that makes you angry, don't kill the messenger. I am just doing what the Lord has asked me to do. Keep in mind that you are reading a book written by a man who, just like you, has committed sin. I'm not writing this book to make friends or to make you like me but that you will walk fully in deliverance in Christ Jesus. When you apply your faith to Godly principles, your mind will be renewed, which will

---

[2] Romans 8:44
[3] John 10:10
[4] 2 Timothy 3:16-17

4

transform your life. If you change the image you have of yourself, you can and will change the outcome. *"As a man thinks, so is he ...."* [5]

NOW, let's get between the sheets.

---

[5] Proverbs 23:7

CHAPTER ONE

God Designed Sex

"Everything has been created through him and for him."
(Colossians 1:16)

God created sex; He determined its design and gave it purpose. He also made it pleasurable and gave it creative power for the procreation of the species. *"And God blessed them, and God said unto them, be fruitful, and multiply, and replenish the earth ...."*[6]

Satan has distorted God's original intentions for sex with his lies! God tells us to guard ourselves from abusing the gift of sex and Satan has spread the lie that more is better! God designed sex for us to enjoy and there are specific reasons to the how and why of an enjoyable sex life. If we are to have a proper understanding of what is God's purpose for sex, we need to go back to the creator — back to God to gain knowledge and a clear understanding of what He wanted sex to provide for us.

Soul ties are created when you have sex.

Since the beginning of time, man has tried to alter God's original intent for life on earth. In Genesis 3,[7] we have the story of Adam and Eve following their own understanding on how to live — they listened to the lies of Satan and were separated from God because of the sin of disobedience. Consequently, sin hindered God's initial plans for man's life on earth. Because sin caused separation from God, Adam and Eve set out on their own journey to explore what life is and how it is supposed to be lived. The consequences of disobedience to God can be seen all around us today. Because of sin-consciousness that entered the earth through Adam's and Eve's disobedience, mankind is dismissive of what God wants and about God's intent for life on earth. In blatant disobedience to God, man is more concerned with living life his way and not according to Godly principles.

---

[6] Genesis 1:28a
[7] Genesis 3

In my counseling experience, the most commonly used reason for not following God's plan for sex is that God's way is boring — people want to have *fun* or *enjoy* life. Sin has dulled God-consciousness in mankind; Satan's lie that life in God is boring has captured the mind. People abuse God's plan for sex because they believe His plan is boring. In other words, they are operating according to the flesh and not according to the Spirit.

However, boredom is not the issue. People lack self-control and, more importantly, they do not have the right knowledge and understanding of God's plan for sexual pleasure. I believe more people would decide to live in accordance with God's plan for sex if they knew that sex is more than a physical act and has spiritual ramifications that could last a life time; that soul ties are created when two come together during sex; and that sex outside God's plan leaves the door open for the devil to come in and touch their bodies and mind with disease and stress. Unfortunately, many people do not know these facts because they get their knowledge of sex from porn videos, dirty magazines, locker room conversations, talk shows or unwise parents and mentors. None of these sources of information will impart the correct information about sex and life. Only the Creator has the correct information about sex and sexual pleasure. The Bible says that the people of God perish (or are destroyed) for their lack of knowledge.[8] The book in your hand will give you the knowledge you need so that, from this day forward, you can make an informed, Holy-Spirit lead decision.

The Bible states that Christ is the one through whom God created everything in heaven and earth: *"For by him all things were created: things in heaven and on earth, visible and invisible, whether thrones or powers or rulers or authorities;* ***all things were created by him and for him"***[9] (emphasis added). Everything was created by a perfect God, including sex.

Sex and the Covenant of Marriage.

God designed sex with specific purposes in mind. First, sex was to take place only between a man and a woman who entered into a sacred

---

[8] Hosea 4:6
[9] Colossians 1:16

7

covenant with Him called marriage – He was to be their God and they were to be husband and wife. In a covenant marriage, the man and woman enter a covenant with each other and with God. God intended that the husband and wife experience sexual union for the first time in marriage; the shedding of blood in this union seals their blood covenant of marriage. The woman bleeds when she loses her virginity and the virginal blood is the seal to the marriage covenant and to the vows made by the wife to her husband and to God. Throughout the Bible, God always seals a covenant with blood. Therefore, God created woman with a hymen so that there would be shedding of blood in a covenant of marriage. (The hymen is a thin membrane which surrounds or partially covers the vaginal opening.) As the husband's penis penetrates the hymen, the hymen stretches and breaks and causes blood to flow onto the man and the woman.

This sexual union of man and woman has spiritual ties to God in heaven. God intended for this blood covenant of marriage to happen only under His covering of blessings. When you fornicate (have sex outside of marriage), a covenant is still made between the man and woman. However, God cannot bless or honor this covenant because it was made outside of His Will. When this happens, the person who has control over the covenant is the god of this world, which is Satan.[10] When you are disobedient to God's plan for sex, you give Satan the right to touch your life and he gladly hinders your Kingdom walk and your destiny in God.

This is true in every area of life. When you do not follow God's instructions for your life, you give the devil permission to touch your life. You may not say this out loud but any time you are disobedient to God's Word, you give room for the enemy to impact your life. Essentially, you are outside of God's covering.

Homosexuality cannot fulfill God's original design for sex.

God designed sex for procreation. Because of the sensual nature of man, God also made sex pleasurable so that procreation would take place in

---

[10] 2 Corinthians 4:4

accordance with His Will. God told Adam and Eve to *"... be fruitful and multiply, and replenish the earth ...."*[11] When He created male and female, He made their sexual organs perfectly complimentary to one another for procreation of the species. The male penis carries the seed and the female vagina receives the male penis so that the seed can be planted inside the womb to fertilize the ovum (egg). Once the male seed is implanted and the egg fertilized, the womb carries the fertilized egg through the developmental stages of life until birth of the fetus. Male and female each have a purpose in bringing forth life into the earth. The male cannot procreate without the female and vice versa. Therefore, homosexuality cannot fulfill God's original purpose for sex because no matter how hard a homosexual couple tries, they need sexual union with someone of the opposite gender in order to procreate. In other words, as same-sex partners, they cannot *"... be fruitful and multiply, and replenish the earth ...."*[12] Lesbians will need the seed of a male and gay males will need the egg and womb of the female in order to create life.

God's plan for procreation is so great that He put the population of the whole earth in the seed of one man joined with the egg of one woman. God could have created billions of people and placed them throughout the earth but He didn't. He created *Adam* and Eve and they started the process of putting billions of people on the earth. Procreation does not occur without sexual union. This reveals the greatness of God's plan and shows that sexual union of the man and woman is part of God's plans for mankind. No matter how small or insignificant something may look, when it is blessed by God it will eventually become great. There are over 7 billion people on earth today and it all started with one man and one woman!

If you can ask God to bless your finances, your health and/or to protect your children, then why wouldn't you also ask Him to touch your sex life if you are married?

God designed sex as an outlet for the expression of our love for one another. He did not only create sex to seal a covenant or to populate the

---

[11] *Supra*
[12] *Supra*

earth, but He also created it for our pleasure and enjoyment! The designs of our sexual organs were created with extra sensory nerves that allow us to experience physical pleasure during sex. God created us with a spirit, soul and physical body and He knew that we would need physical pleasure to truly enjoy life here on earth. God wanted us to enjoy our husbands and wives physically because we live in a physical world. We grow closer to our spouses when we have sex; this happens physically and spiritually. Of course, the best part about God's design is that He created the orgasm for our *total pleasure* during sex.

This sensual pleasure during sex is what drives the human race in its sexual desires. Because of the dullness of our God-consciousness due to sin, humans do not care about the covenant of God or about reproducing life; people just want to *'feel good'* like Halle Berry in the movie Monsters Ball. *"Feeling good"* is what gets people in trouble with STD's, unwanted pregnancies and life-long soul ties. Satan knows that sex outside of God's Will is a mere reflection of what God wants for us. I can tell you from personal experience that sex outside of marriage does not compare to sex within the covering of God. I have had sex with hundreds of women in my life and none of those experiences can even compare to what my Wife and I have shared in pleasurable sex. This may seem to be impossible but let me be the first to tell you that when God is a part of anything in our lives they work out much better than when He is not involved. This includes our sex lives.

Many in the church believe God has nothing to do with the marriage bed but this is untrue and irresponsible thinking. God desires to lead us in every area of life,[13] including in the bedroom. Now, I am not saying that my Wife and I listen to gospel music during sex. But we do pray about our sex life and ask the Holy Spirit to lead us in pleasing one another sexually. Think about it this way: If you ask God to bless your finances, your health and/or to protect your children, then why would you not ask Him to touch your sex life if you are married? Let's not become so spiritual we are no earthly good in the bedroom to our husbands and wives. The Bible even

---

[13] Proverbs 3:5-6

speaks to how important is the sexual act in marriage when he tells us not to deprive one another of sex: *"Do not deprive each other of sexual relations, unless you both agree to refrain from sexual intimacy for a limited time so you can give yourselves more completely to prayer. Afterward, you should come together again so that Satan won't be able to tempt you because of your lack of self-control."*[14]

In today's sexual environment, many of us marry AFTER having had sexual involvements. Therefore, we often are not virgins when we marry. Early in my marriage, I thought what I did in my lust relationships could be done in my marriage bed but I was sadly mistaken. I put my marriage relationship in jeopardy wanting some of the things that I had enjoyed in my sinful lifestyle. I had to ask God to deliver me from lustful desires! Asking God's direction and blessing in sexual relationship in marriage is a very wise thing to do. The marriage covenant in God is based on love, not lust and, therefore, the marriage bed in this covenant is based on love, not lust. We must be careful not to confuse the two because it can result in damage to our marriage relationships.

Many of the sexual practices I enjoyed in lust will be discussed later in the book. Praise God for deliverance and for a right sexual relationship with my beautiful Wife!! We now enjoy a much more fulfilling sex life and, as I mentioned earlier, I am a better lover for my Wife. God wanted my Wife and me to enjoy sex.

If you are married, I believe that when you finish reading this book you will experience a new and more vibrant sex life with your spouse. You will also learn how to avoid many of the pitfalls of Satan and will know what to expect when you are married. You will be better prepared to please your spouse and to create a more satisfying love relationship.

As you can see, God's design for sex is much different than what the TV or your friends tell you. God is a God of purpose and everything He created He created with a purpose in mind. We must have a clear understanding of what is God's purpose for everything in life because **when purpose is unknown, abuse is inevitable**.

---

[14] 1 Corinthians 7:5 (NLT)

CHAPTER TWO

Naughty by Nature: Pornography & Masturbation

"For all that is in the world, the lust of the flesh, and the lust of the eyes, and the pride of life,
is not of the Father, but is of the world."
(1 John 2:16)

It's wrong to watch others have sex, whether it's hard-core porn or love scenes in a movie. Jesus said that if you look upon a woman (or person you're not married to) with lust you have sinned.[15] It's also wrong to have sex with ourselves. No matter what so-called "experts" say about the benefits of masturbation, God created man to be sexually intimate only with his wife, and vice versa, so that the two would become one in mind, body and spirit.[16]

A recent article in a popular men's health magazine stated that "Masturbation is part of a healthy sex life. It's totally safe and harmless. It's healthier than brushing your teeth every day."[17] This is just not true! The truth is that we were not fashioned to satisfy ourselves by having sex with our hands or other objects. The referenced article from Men'sHealth News online intimates that masturbation helps prevent cancer and keeps the immune system up. In order to support ridiculous claims, the article cites studies on cancer prevention and the immune system that herald frequent ejaculation to prevent cancer and for a healthy immune system. God is perfect and thorough. When we were designed by God, He took into consideration that we would have times in our lives that we would not be married and, therefore, prohibited from having sex. God gave the body the ability to release on its own, without outside influence. Satan can use doctors and scientists to perpetuate his lies and to further anesthetize to the truth in God's Word. Because of lies spread by these medical and scientific experts, Christians are masturbating so they don't get cancer. Do you see

---

[15] Matthew 5:28
[16] Matthew 19:4-6
[17] Reyes, M. (Dec 29, 2011), 5 Health Benefits of Masturbation, *Men'sHealth News* (online), retrieved from
http://news.menshealth.com/masturbate-every-day/2011/12/29/

how ridiculous that sounds? The truth is that we are healed by the Blood Jesus shed for us, not by pleasing ourselves sexually.[18]

Doctors, scientists and philosophers continually change their opinion and opinions vary between ages and cultures. Financial advisor, Dave Ramsey said: "I've heard it said that if you tell a lie often enough, loud enough and long enough, it will become accepted as a fact. Repetition, volume and longevity will twist and turn a myth or a lie into a commonly accepted way of doing things."[19] Societal views are ever evolving and changing as new discoveries are made and new theories are fashioned. However, the Word of God never changes; it is always constant and always true. Doctors call their profession a practice because in medicine little is known as an absolute certainty. The opinions of mere men pale in comparison to God's superior knowledge and wisdom. I love Isaiah 45:13-16 when it says: *"Who is able to advise the Spirit of the LORD? Who knows enough to be his teacher or counselor? Has the LORD ever needed anyone's advice? Does he need instruction about what is good or what is best? No, for all the nations of the world are nothing in comparison with him. They are but a drop in the bucket, dust on the scales. He picks up the islands as though they had no weight at all."*[20] God does not need advice or instruction from His creation!

It is no surprise that pornography is a billion dollar industry in which many have been caught up. Both pornography and masturbation are tools of Satan to bring strongholds into our lives. A stronghold is a real spiritual fortress that has you captured and locked inside sin, and will keep you from living freely in Christ.

Pornography and masturbation are spiritual because they extend from the invisible realm and from the imagination. With both, you imagine having sex with someone who is not usually present at the time. We know from God's Word that the invisible is more real than the physical (natural) realm in which we spend a majority of our time.[21] The spiritual realm is

---

[18] Exodus 15:26
[19] Ramsey, D (2009 ed). *The total money makeover: A proven plan for financial fitness.* Nashville, TN: Thomas Nelson Publishers
[20] Isaiah 40:13-16 (NLT)

both our origin and where God Himself abides. Our faith in God and our fear of the unknown originate from this unseen realm.

God gave us the power to create by using our imagination. Without the capacity to imagine, we would be restricted in our abilities. Our imagination has given us the technological and medical advancements we have today. We move from our present to our future with our imagination. In Hebrews 11, it is clear that each Patriarch made decisions based on what they saw in the unseen realm.[22] It is the same for us. God dealt with Abraham, Jacob and Joseph through the imagination and He deals the same with us.[23]

By nature, the mind is wicked and disobedient and creates imaginations contrary to the good and perfect Will of God.[24]

Our imaginations were never intended for pornography and masturbation. The Bible clearly conveys what we are to think about, "... *whatever is **true**, whatever is noble, whatever is right, whatever is **pure**, whatever is lovely, whatever is admirable--if anything is excellent or praiseworthy--think about such things*" (emphasis added).[25] The adjectives used in Philippians 4:8 are descriptions of God Himself. In addition, we are told to meditate on the Word of God day and night continually.[26] These behaviors become second-nature to the Believer when his mind is renewed by the Word of God. In this context, the word "renewed" means the mind is "renovated" so that the old ideals are ripped out and replaced with God's standards and principles.

After the fall of man, the mind is wicked and disobedient and easily capable of creating imaginations that are contrary to the good and perfect Will of God. The sinful desires of our hearts cause us to demean our bodies and lead us to do things with our body never intended by God. Our wicked nature and dark hearts suppress God's truth. Even those who claim to be

---

[21] Hebrews 11:6
[22] Hebrews 11:13
[23] Read Genesis 15, Genesis 28 and Genesis 37
[24] Genesis 6:5
[25] Philippians 4:8
[26] Joshua 1:8

followers of Christ watch lust-filled cinema, pornography and resort to autoeroticism. Those that claim to be wise are, in fact, fools when they contradict God's Word. The world is so corrupt that it cannot receive this Word that I am teaching. Anyone who rejects this Word does so because they are locked in something that the flesh has orchestrated. We must *"live by the Spirit, and you will not gratify the desires of the sinful nature. For the sinful nature desires what is contrary to the Spirit and the Spirit what is contrary to the sinful nature. They are in conflict with each other, so that you do not do what you want."*[27] Our flesh will never agree with the Spirit of God.

Your mind is the gateway for both Satan and God.

When we engage in the spiritual realm, we are opening doors for God or the enemy to work through. God gave us the authority to rule the earth and He interferes in our ruling when we allow Him to do so. This is typically accomplished through prayer and speaking or obeying God's Word in faith. When we imagine ourselves having sex with the person on the screen, the portal to the spiritual realm opens. However, it is a door for the enemy to walk through and not God. When watching pornography or masturbating, you are giving Satan permission to access your life. I'm sure you've heard the saying that your mind is the battlefield. Well, Satan wants your mind because he then gains the right of entry to your faith.[28] In the same way, God desires for the Word to be preached to you so that He can take over your mind so that His Word directs every part of your life.[29]

The mind is so powerful that by controlling your mind you can have an orgasm without touching yourself. You cannot have an orgasm when masturbating without thinking about something to erotically stimulate the mind. Whatever you think about when you masturbate, that is what you are conjuring up. To conjure means to pull from the invisible realm and bring into the natural realm. When you conjure, something comes through a spiritual portal. I have lain in bed touching myself, thinking of someone in my past and the phone rings; that person is on the other end. This happens

---

[27] Galatians 5:16-17
[28] Ephesians 6:16
[29] Romans 12:2

because I have reached out at them and they felt me pull at them in the spirit. Your imagination is powerful and real. Just like God imagined the world and spoke it into instantaneous existence, we were created in His image to have the power to bring things into existence from our imagination.

With AIDS and HIV rampant in our society, many argue that masturbation is a good way to practice safe sex. That also is a trick of the enemy. Notice that the word masturbate has both the word *master* and the word *bate* in it, although this may be coincidental as the word literally means to release at a high speed. Satan is called the master of the air.[30] Just as we are completely immersed in air and unable to avoid it, we also cannot avoid Satan's influence upon the earth. His influence has bated many Christians in a deceptive trap because masturbation keeps the mind focused on what you're not getting — SEX.

Your sex drive has to be put to sleep.

When you are not married but have a sexual past, your sex drive has to be put to sleep. You have to put that 'baby' to bed. A sleeping baby makes no noise but a baby that is awake will place demands on you and require your attention. Once you start to have sex, you have to surrender to God to stop because you were never designed to stop having sex. In order to rein in your sex drive, you have to surrender to God by first admitting you cannot do it without Him. Your confession may sound something like this: "Lord, I know I need to stop masturbating and watching porn but I cannot stop. Please help me." When you surrender to Him in that way, He will help you! 1 John 1:8-10 says: *"If we claim to be without sin, we deceive ourselves and the truth is not in us. If we confess our sins, he is faithful and just and will forgive us our sins and purify us from all unrighteousness. If we claim we have not sinned, we make him out to be a liar and his word has no place in our lives."*[31]

In order to gain victory, you must surrender your sexuality to God by first admitting (confessing) to Him that your sexuality does not meet His

---

[30] Ephesians 2:2
[31] 1 John 1:8-10

16

standards. Don't be embarrassed about discussing your sexuality with God because he knows you inside and out.[32] When we talk about our faults, He is fair (rightly just) in pardoning our short comings. That means that God completely erases them and does not hold them against us. He also purifies us when we talk to Him about our blunders. Trust the Word, Child of God. Once you talk to Him, purification is taking place whether deliverance is instantaneous or over a period of time. It's when we don't admit we have a problem or that we need help that we are stuck in our sin.

The body goes through withdrawal from both porn and masturbation similar to the withdrawal associated with drug or alcohol use. You are fighting an addiction and it can be an uncomfortable and draining battle both mentally and physically. Do not be discouraged and give up if you fall. There may be some instances you find yourself rolled up in a ball crying, kicking and screaming or rocking yourself back and forth just to keep yourself from watching porn or masturbating. With a made up mind and the power of the Holy Ghost, the addiction will weaken.

As humans, we are heavily influenced by our environments. The "hu" in human derives from the word humus, which means dirt. The "man" in human means spirit being. We are a spirit being in dirt (clay). When it comes to sexual addictions, you have sown wrong desires into dirt. Some of you have sown these wrong desires for years and, therefore, your mind and body are accustomed to these desires. Just like in the natural, whatever you plant and cultivate in dirt will take root and grow. You must change your environment and avoid lustful movies and websites. Create a new atmosphere with praise, worship and the Word of God. If you focus on changing the images in your mind to images that are true, noble, right, pure, lovely and admirable, you will become these things. The Bible says whatever you think about you will become.[33]

If you change the image, you will change the outcome.

---

[32] Matthew 10:30 and Acts 15:8
[33] Proverbs 23:7

17

There are a couple principles that I really need you to get. The principles which I am about to speak derive from scriptures that we have heard so often that they have almost become cliché. But I really need you to grasp what I'm saying here because they are truths that will bring you into freedom.

First, the Bible says in Matthew 6 to make the Kingdom of God the first priority in your life. So, do this for me. Take a quick examination of what you spend the majority of your money on, the majority of your time doing, the area you focus your talents and skill on the most and what you spend most of your time talking about. If any one of these answers is not the Kingdom of God, you have a good idea where to start asking God to help you make some changes. Why? One way to break addiction is to shift your focus from the problem to the Will of God. When you transfer your attention to the Kingdom, you have now shifted your focus from the problem. In essence, the Kingdom consists of the very thought, will and decrees of the King. When you focus on the Kingdom, you are paying attention to the King as well. We often make our problems and issues so large that God has become small. We have made these problems and issues idols in our lives. An idol is anything you place before God.

The Bible says *"let us throw off everything that hinders and the sin that so easily entangles, and let us run with perseverance the race marked out for us. Let us fix our eyes on Jesus, the author and perfecter of our faith ...."*[34] You cannot complete the assignment God has for your life with weights on. Weights are hindrances. Weights are traps structured by your own desires.[35]

Second, in conjunction with shifting your focus to the Kingdom, you also need to get in the Word like never before to break sexual bondage in your life. The Word says how can a man be cleansed but by the Word of God?[36] The Word is a cleansing agent. When you meditate on and study the Word, it is truth poured into your mind to wash away the untruths (the lies of Satan). The reason a man continues in alcoholism is because of what he

---

[34] Hebrews 12:1-2
[35] James 1:14
[36] Psalms 119:9

thinks of himself. The reason you might continue to masturbate or to watch porn is because of what you think of you. You have to change your image to change your outcome. The Word renews your mind so that you think what God thinks of you. This is very, very important to understand. We become what we think in our minds.

Addiction to pornography and to masturbation is like drug addiction. Just as a drug user will progress to stronger drugs, the sex addicted will progress to more hard-core sexual activities and sexual perversion. In order to orgasm while watching porn or while masturbating, you have to channel (i.e., conjure up) something that you actually want to have in reality. Eventually your desire will bring you closer and closer to creating this reality. This is always the case; sin is progressive. You will eventually need to fulfill your sexual fantasies. Your imagination takes you places whether good or bad. The Bible says that what a person thinks about he will become.[37] Whatever you are thinking on is going to be the end of you. If you are thinking about someone else's wife as you masturbate, adultery will eventually set in and you will become an adulterer. If you constantly masturbate to homosexual pornography, you will eventually make those fantasies a reality when the opportunity presents itself.

---

[37] Proverbs 23:7

CHAPTER THREE

The G^od Spot: Married Sex

"For this reason a man shall leave his father and his mother, and be joined to his wife; and they shall become one flesh."
(Genesis 2:24)

Marriage between a man and a woman is an institution that God stands behind. It is an institution that is honorable in His presence and so is the love-making in marriage. God's principles are always applicable, even in married sex. People will often use Hebrews 13:4 as a license to do any and everything in the bedroom. Hebrews 13:4 says: *"Marriage is honorable among all, and the bed undefiled."*[38] The Godly principle in this scripture cautions us against breaking our covenant through adultery and fornication whereby we defile the marriage bed. What this scripture is NOT saying is that everything that married couples might do in the bedroom is acceptable to God. Once again, God's principles are unchanging and always relevant. Satan's lies are designed to twist the Word of God so that we pervert our relationships.

We have listened to the lies of Satan for so long that we do not recognize that Hebrews 13:4 cautions us to **not** defile the marriage bed with un-Godly sexual perversion. Take, for example, erotic asphyxiation and anal sex. (Erotic asphyxiation is the intentional restriction of oxygen to the brain for sexual arousal by choking your sex partner.[39]) These perverse sexual acts abuse the body, which is the temple of the Holy Spirit. Therefore, they go against Godly principles. No matter how much these sexual perversions get you off, they are not to be a part of the marriage bed!

If our sexual intercourse dishonors God, we also defile the marriage bed. During anal sex, the wife is being ruptured anally and her body is

---

[38] Hebrews 13:4
[39] See http://en.wikipedia.org/wiki/Erotic_asphyxiation

being abused. Abuse of the body is abuse of the temple of the Holy Spirit and dishonors God.[40] The marriage bed is defiled.

You might ask why or how the woman's body is being abused during anal sex. It is being abused because God's purpose for the anus is **not** for sexual intercourse. God structured the tissue around the sphincter muscle very delicately and it tears easily. When the sphincter tears, it is painful. There is also very little natural lubrication for penetration of the anus. But, most importantly, feces come out of the anus. The function of the anus is for elimination and not for receiving the penis or for taking anything in! Furthermore, the feces found in the anal canal are to be eliminated from the body and contain germs that could cause infection in the penis and in the vagina. It is unhealthy to spread those feces to other parts of the body! Common sense tells us that God does not want us to enter through the anus. Anal sex does not honor God in any way and, therefore, defiles the marriage bed.

When purpose is unknown, abuse is inevitable.

In Romans 1:21 it says *"And they began to think up foolish ideas of what God was like."*[41] Mankind has now come up with the bright idea that it is okay with God that we put objects where waste comes out of the body He created! (For those of you who respond here that blood comes out of a woman's vagina, yes that is true. But that occurs once a month and you are not to have sex during menstruation.) Whether you want to call it a sin or not, the anus was made to eliminate waste from the body and not to take in. You'll hear me say this a lot: When purpose is unknown, abuse is inevitable. Romans 1:21 continues with *"The result was that their minds became dark and confused."*[42]

Look at what happens when we come up with foolish ideas; we jeopardize body and health. Believing the lies of Satan, we have reasoned in our own mind that in the marriage bed God would honor masturbation,

---

[40] 1 Corinthians 6:19
[41] Romans 1:21
[42] *Id.*

would honor watching porn, would honor choking one another and sticking the penis, or foreign objects in our anus. On top of that, in the name of medicine and science, we have reasoned that masturbation is okay with God because it is for our health. That is truly leaning to our own understanding!! Are you beginning to understand and recognize that we have come so far from God's original design for sex that we are deceived in our own thinking? The enemy has entered our bedrooms while using the Word of God to justify sexual abuse.

God is not a God of abuse, no matter how society wants to portray Him. God is not responsible for the abuse, hurt and anguish in the world. We have reasoned in our own minds and have rejected the wise counsel of God's Word while, at the same time, accepting the twisted lies of Satan. Our decision to reject and disobey God is what has damaged our communities and our quality of life, including our sex lives. God's plans "are to prosper you and not to harm you, plans to give you hope and a future."[43] When we give Satan room in any area of our lives we hinder God's plans for us. We must make a conscious choice to follow the leading of the Spirit of God. God uses marriage in his plans to bring Himself glory and for the growth of His kingdom.

As two come together they become one spiritually, mentally and physically.

The marriage bed is about love, intimacy and oneness. The marriage bed represents the relationship that we are to have with Christ. When we receive Him as Lord of our Lives and Savior of our Spirits, we unite with Him. As we commune with Him we are to become one with Him. We are to know Christ intimately. We are to allow Him to touch areas that only He, the Lover of our Souls, should touch. As two come together in the marriage bed, they unite spiritually, mentally and physically. When the man climaxes, everything in him is received by the woman; the man's DNA (his very makeup) is received by the woman. The woman receives and accepts the man wholeheartedly when he climaxes. When the woman receives the man she is saying, "There is nothing about you I don't want; I want it all."

---

[43] Jeremiah 29:11

The woman is agreeing to receive everything about the man, and the man is agreeing to give all of him to the woman. This intimate agreement is part of the covenant of marriage, which is a mimic of the covenant we have with God. In our covenant with God, He wants us to give all of ourselves to Him; everything we have, everything we are and everything we are not. This is a bond that goes beyond anything else. In the covenant of marriage in which husband and wife operate with the mind of Christ, they desire that same bond with one another that is had with a covenant with God. Whether you are single, married or divorced, I suggest that you get your hands on all the information you can on covenant so that you can have a better understanding of marriage and what God wants to take place in marriage.

In Genesis 2:24, the Bible uses the word cleave to describe the uniting that takes place between husband and wife. The word cleave in the Hebrew is dabaq (daw-bak'), meaning to cling, stick, stay close, keep close, stick to, stick with, follow closely, join to and to overtake. In the Garden of Eden, Satan used his lies and schemes to separate and destroy dabaq in the marriage of Adam and Eve and is still on the same assignment today. The Bible says in Amos 3:3: *"Do two walk together unless they have agreed to do so?"*[44] In order for our marriages to reach destiny and fulfill the assignments God has for us, we must be in complete agreement with our spouses. God wants no division in marriage; He wants us perfectly united in mind and thought.[45] He wants His love, His spirit and His purpose as the posture in our marriages.[46] Dabaq extends from the mind set of Christ, is of great value and worth fighting for. Having the mind of Christ means we look at life from our Savior's point of view, with His values and His desires in mind. Having the mind of Christ means thinking God's thoughts and not thinking as the world thinks.

Without understanding the depths of interaction in sexual intercourse, the likely result will be to abuse sex and to take God's design for granted. When we join our body with another in sex, the oneness of our minds opens

---

[44] Amos 3:3
[45] 1 Corinthians 1:10
[46] Philippians 2:1-3

a portal in the spirit realm to allow our spiritual bodies to intertwine. (Remember that the mind is the key to the invisible realm.) Take a moment to think back to a time you made love to someone for the first time. If you were conscious of it, there was a feeling of warmth that came over you as you made love. That warm feeling was the merging and intertwining of two spirits; you were becoming one with the other. In our ignorance, we have made sex a dirty word. We have perverted sex and turned it into something other than for what God designed. The more people you sleep with, the more spirits with which your spirit interlocks. In God's original design, He only intended for us to have sex with one person in our life time and that one person was to be our life-long marriage partner. We were never supposed to separate outside of death. Once you have sex with someone, you cannot go back to the way you were before you joined with them. You have already exchanged spirits and DNA. You have exchanged with that person your very essence.

In many marriages today, spouses coexist in the same house but do not experience God's best. The main problem with marriage today is that God is not the focal point. Even if you enjoy good sex in your marriage, that does not guarantee a good marriage. The main purpose for marriage is to produce for the Kingdom of God in the spiritual and in the natural. In God's plan, the children of a marriage are to be taught to serve God with their whole heart and with their very lives.

If people really honored God and understood God's purpose for marriage, there would be less dishonor of God in marriage. A godly marriage is unto the Lord and things like same-sex marriage and wife-swapping do not honor God. A same-sex marriage is subject to Satan because it goes against God's original design. The practice of wife swapping also dishonors God. Any man who can hand his wife over to another man to have sex with her does not have the mind of Christ or even love for his wife. God is love and you cannot have love without God. Unfortunately, many marriages today are not based on love. When you follow the principles of God and are affecting the Kingdom, you will experience a successful marriage.

Married sex is not boring… God endorses hot and satisfying sex!

Married sex is a gift that was given for reproduction, covenant and an outlet for passion! Married sex is not boring and was never intended to be boring. Dull and boring sex in a marriage is a trick of the enemy to destroy the marriage. In marriage, God endorses and encourages hot and satisfying sex! In fact, part of being in God's will is having a fulfilling sex life in marriage.

Many factors may come into play to keep sex from being pleasurable. A few examples are personal feelings, issues from childhood and experiences of abuse or unsatisfying sexual intercourse in the past with others. All of these factors will cause discord in the marriage relationship if the marriage partners do not heal from the memories of these experiences. A lack of unity in the marriage relationship will affect sexual pleasure. In order to fix the sexual relationship and increase sexual pleasure, you have to let God heal your brokenness with His Word.

If you don't enjoy the sex in your marriage you have to get your mind right. YOU have to make the commitment to release the thoughts, habits and events that hinder your sex life. You and your spouse must develop a like mind. Sexual passion and pleasure, like everything else, begins in the mind. Communicate! Talk to one another about what each of you likes and explore one another sexually. Take the time to learn how to satisfy one another and how each can let the other give sexual pleasure. You can retrain your mind and body to enjoy your spouse if you are determined to do so. It is not all about you but about together creating a satisfying, enjoyable and exciting sex life with your spouse. After time, prayer and patience, you will develop an intimacy with your spouse that will cause the passion in your love-making to increase. Do not allow Satan to have any ground in your marriage. It takes work to have a good marriage and to have a satisfying sexual relationship in marriage.

In some instances, one partner may be uncomfortable with certain sexual activities. In this case, the mate with reservations should pray and make efforts to fulfill the other's request. While one is learning and working to accommodate the other's request, the requesting spouse should make every effort to encourage and show appreciation for their spouse's efforts, even if those efforts are, initially, disappointing. As you work together, your spouse will learn how to please you. Never pressure your spouse because the goal is for both of you to enjoy doing what pleases the other. This is a delicate area and Satan loves to attack weaknesses and bring about division. Be submissive to one another with a constant and consistent give and take on both sides. Each of you should clothe yourselves with compassion, kindness, humility, gentleness and patience.[47] When you study covenant, you will find that the parties to the covenant vow that each have access to all that they have. Covenant partners share everything but never abuse that right of access.

"I don't want him to touch me like that"

"*... Each man should have his own wife, and each woman her own husband. The husband should fulfill his marital duty to his wife, and likewise the wife to her husband. The wife's body does not belong to her alone but also to her husband. In the same way, the husband's body does not belong to him alone but also to his wife. Do not deprive each other except by mutual consent and for a time, so that you may devote yourselves to prayer. Then come together again so that Satan will not tempt you because of your lack of self-control.*"[48] (Emphasis added.)

As mentioned previously, you should let God heal you of past abuse BEFORE marrying. There are women and men clinging to the memories of abuse and bad sexual experiences and bringing those memories into the marriage. I have counseled some who say, "I don't want him to touch me like that because so-and-so touched me like that." It is wrong for a person that has suffered abuse to come into a marriage knowing they have not been healed from past hurts. You have begged and pleaded with God for a spouse and now you reject what was given to you. I may not be talking to everybody, but I know I'm talking to somebody. Write this down, because I

---

[47] Colossians 3:12
[48] 1 Corinthians 7:2-5

need you to get this. "Rejecting my spouse will destroy my marriage!" Destruction is Satan's job; don't allow him to use you.

Did you get that? **Never** show your spouse that you are disgusted by them or uninterested in them. If he taps you on your shoulder, take a Tylenol and roll over! As a man, I want to be reverenced by my wife. I want to be held in a position of honor by my wife. If all I'm getting from my wife is rejection, I will eventually stop asking her for anything. When the wife regularly rejects her husband's advances, he will take the rejection as indicative that he is not in a primary position in the wife's heart and mind. Like mindedness goes out the door at that point, which further affects marital intimacy. However, sexual desire is still there because that's how God designed us. Unfulfilled sexual desires in marriage lead to one or the other spouse seeking fulfillment outside of the marriage partner, which is adultery. The only time you and your spouse should not be having sex with one another is when you <u>both</u> have agreed to submit yourselves to prayer and fasting. If you don't want everything that comes with having a spouse, don't get married.

There are many Christian marriages are ending in divorce because someone cheated. It is often the case that the person stepped outside of the marriage because their spouse did not keep the sexual area locked down. There also may be other needs not being met. Some of you may want to make excuses for infidelity in marriage due to sexual dissatisfaction. However, the bottom line is that we need to let God heal us BEFORE marrying. If you are already married, surrender to God and let Him heal you. Read 1 Corinthians 7:1-5 again. Satan comes to tempt when there has been no sex for a certain period of time. Marriage needs good sex regularly for cleaving to take place.

It is also inadvisable and generally wrong to marry if you are a person accustomed to more than one sexual partner at one time, are used to several sexual partners in a short period of time or used to homosexual encounters. One person cannot give you the same level of sexual activity as, let's say, twenty can give you. Trust me! Let God heal you first before marrying.

I was a guy who was used to sexing more than one woman at a time and having sexual intercourse several times in a day, every day. I had a fight in the beginning of my marriage because I was used to my sexual needs being met at all times of the day by many (women) sexual partners. I was unrealistic in expecting a sexual appetite that I had developed in lustful relationships to be met by one woman. It was unfair to my wife to place a sexual demand on her that was previously being met by more than one sexual partner! I had unfair and unrealistic expectations. Your spouse is required to satisfy you sexually but there must be a balance. If you and your spouse are always in the bedroom having sex, there is no time to work on the vision God has given you and your marriage is out of line with His Will.

It is very frustrating when you have dated and had many sexual partners and now you are trying to bring it all in and sex only one person. Making things click in your marriage can be a challenge. You must create a plan (a strategy) for success in your sexual life with your spouse or you plan to fail. I will give some thoughts on this later in this chapter.

If you are experiencing unfulfilled sexual gratification or any problems in your marriage related to sex, you have to talk with your spouse about what in your past could be affecting your sexual interactions. You don't have to be detailed and graphic but you must be honest – especially honest with yourself. For example, tell your spouse that you have been with other sexual partners but that you want and need her/him to be the one who can satisfy your sexual needs. It may not be easy at first but, with focus and prayer, you and your spouse will develop the right strategy and will reach the level of intimacy God desires in a marriage. If the two of you were not saved when you married, you can create an honorable marriage now that the two of you are saved. Get the mind of Christ and bring it in. If one of you is not serving the Lord, it will be tough. You will have to do spiritual warfare to get that other one in place.

A man needs two things to get him going; visual stimuli and respect.

The strategy to improve your sex life may include the wife wearing certain outfits that her husband likes. Perhaps the two of you could shop for these items together. A man needs two things to get him going — visual stimuli and respect. The woman's responsibility is to look good for her husband so as to make a statement that he is **The Man**. When a man is made to feel like a man, his body will respond like a man.

Women, you may think that what I am saying indicates that a man does not need love. A man does want and need love, just like you do. God made man to love and he gave the man woman to love him and to be loved by him. We are all getting love coming down from God. Paul did not emphasize woman loving a man because, generally, if a woman respects a man, there is love mixed with it. When a man is in the right place with God, he is loved. As a Woman of God being in a marriage with a man that does not have a relationship with the Lord can be difficult. Especially, if you are a woman serving the Lord because it's hard to be satisfied with less than God's best. The man needs to shift his focus to his woman and get his mind off of the fantasies. Keep your mind in the right place.

Women need love…overtake her with love.

Women need love. Men, you have to show your woman that you love her. Overtake her with love and most women will keep you sexually satisfied for years as well as build a satisfying marriage relationship with you. A man's strategy for loving on his wife might be to regularly flirt with her and tell her she looks good. You might also slap your wife on the backside when she passes you in the kitchen or whisper you love her softly in her ear and walk out the room. This is a form of flirting.

In marriage, flirting should be constant. In fact, to those I counsel I call flirting sexual communication or foreplay. Sexual communication is great because it opens the doors for both verbal and nonverbal communication. It stimulates the sex in the bedroom because you are telling your spouse what you want from them and how you feel about them without saying it outright. By the time you get to the bedroom she is ready for you. Recently, my wife and I were in a meeting with my staff and I shot her a text message saying "You look sexy; I want that." I got a smile from her in the meeting and something even better later on.

Those that have learned to respond to themselves are leaving their spouse at a loss.

Those that have become accustomed to their own touch or sex toys will struggle with enjoying sex in marriage as it was intended by God. Those that have learned to respond to themselves are leaving their spouse at a loss. (Even a future spouse if you are not yet married.) The spouse will be unable to be the one and only person that brings you to sexual climax. Often women become accustomed to toys so large that their husbands just cannot compete. The use of sexual toys is unfair to both the husband and the sexual relationship. When God designed sex, he did not intend toys to be used for sexual gratification. The man's penis was designed to enter the woman's vagina and the woman's vagina was designed to receive the man's penis and should it fit like a hand in glove.

Whether you are married or not, if you have suffered sexual abuse or have had sexual relations before marriage, let God heal you of these past relationships, hurt and abuse before marrying. Speak the Word over yourself, over your spouse and over your situation, as the words you speak will change the identity and characteristics of your marriage. We do what we do in life based on what was done in our past. You have to let go of the past in order to have a satisfying marriage relationship with the man or woman of your future. True healing brings deliverance. If you have discovered that you are not having sex in your marriage according to God's original design, you and your spouse should seek the Lord for healing. Start practicing correct marital sex. It may take time and work to come into oneness and wholeness but you will get it. Your spouse and your marriage are worth it!!

CHAPTER FOUR

First Base: Flirting and Kissing

"Simply let your 'Yes' be 'Yes,' and your 'No,' 'No;'
anything beyond this comes from the evil one."
(Matthew 5:37)

We all have done it. Many of us started flirting at five years old with our first boyfriend or girlfriend. Some of us waited until we got to high school to flirt. Still others of us did not flirt until we were adults. But at some point or another we have all flirted.

Flirting is so common in the US that when people don't do it they are thought to have something wrong with them. Flirting is misleading and not sincere if you don't mean it. The Merriam-Webster dictionary online defines flirting as "2.a. to behave amorously without serious intent; 2.b. to show superficial or casual interest or liking."[49] The point here is that flirting is deception; it stems from the flesh and is not genuine. The flirtatious acts usually projects lustful images to the person with whom you're flirting. The flirt creates a sensual environment with their words in which Satan can freely operate. The people flirted with often get caught in the web of words spoken. Flirting is also seduction because it gets the person thinking sexually about the person flirting with them. If the person is not married to you, they should not be thinking of you sexually!

When married, flirting with your spouse is like foreplay. Outside of the marriage relationship, flirting is deception.

If you have a flirtatious personality, it is most likely something you have developed through years of saying what you need to say to get what you want. Women who do not flirt with men are said to have an attitude. Men who do not flirt with an attractive woman are thought to be gay. The person who flirts needs to have the mind renewed by the Word of God.

---

[49] Merriam-Webster Online Dictionary (2013). Retrieved from http://www.merriam-webster.com/dictionary/flirting

Why is flirting so important to our culture? Why does it seem to be necessary to be sexually successful with the opposite sex? Why is something thought to be wrong with the person who does not participate in flirtatious behavior? Let's explore what the Bible says about flirting to answer these questions.

Scientists say that flirting is natural and a healthy part of finding a mate. They say that flirting is done by animals to show interest and to show strength in child bearing. Examples from the animal kingdom are often used to justify flirting among humans. For example, male lions shake their mane to attract a mate; peacocks and other birds display bright feathers to attract a mate. These examples are cited by scientists to show that animals flirt for the purpose of choosing a mate. Then, scientists hypothesize that humans engage in similar actions for similar reasons. Furthermore, scientists speculate that the limbic system in the human body will kick into gear when we find someone to whom we are attracted. According to Wikipedia.com, the limbic system "is a complex set of brain structures that lies on both sides of the thalamus, right under the cerebrum. It appears to be primarily responsible for our emotional life, and has a great deal to do with the formation of memories."[50] The limbic system is, therefore, believed to be the driving force by which we respond to people to whom we are attracted, as well as causes the logical mind to take a back seat to our more primal side.[51]

As Kingdom Citizens, we should not accept what the scientists of the world say as truth without critically evaluating and comparing it to what God says in His Word. Many scientists have good intentions but good intentions can still be wrong if the result opposes the Word of God. It would be a sweeping generalization fallacy of logic for scientists to conclude that homo sapiens (humans) would act in the same way as another species!! Even lions and peacocks are considered different species but scientists want to classify their mating habits similarly and, then, claim they are the same as homo sapiens. This is a stretch of the imagination and an example of leaning to our own understanding. It is mere speculation to hypothesize that flirting

[50] Wikipedia.com (21 Feb 2013). Retrieved from http://en.wikipedia.org/wiki/Limbic_system
[51] Id.

is natural to homo sapiens because lions shake their mane and peacocks spread colorful feathers.

Flirting is discussed in the Bible as being sin. (Remember, however, that we are talking about flirting with someone other than your spouse. Flirting with your spouse is not sin but a way to stimulate sexual desires; I call it foreplay.) Scientists associate flirting with the limbic system and our emotions. However, the Bible tells us not to be led by our emotions but by God's Word and by His Spirit.[52] Emotions are tied to the sinful nature, which entered the world because of the fall of Adam and Eve in the Garden of Eden.[53] Our emotions change with the wind and cannot be trusted, and our emotions direct us to what is pleasing to the flesh. The Bible says that the flesh is enmity to the Spirit of God.[54]

Apostle Paul writes in the New Testament that we should be led by the Spirit of God so that we don't satisfy the desires of the flesh.[55] The word flesh means sinful nature or carnal mindset. Our emotions are directly tied to the sinful nature and to the flesh. Being led by the flesh will cause a separation from God, and will manifest as things like fear, anger, bitterness or sorrow. Expressing emotion is not sinful; however, being led by emotions is in direct opposition to being led by the Spirit of God. To be led by the Spirit is to take on the mind of Christ.[56] When we are led by the Spirit, we will not please our flesh (sinful nature), but will do those things pleasing to God.

Flirting is quite simply a lie; flirting is deception.

Flirting is said to be harmless but rarely is. Let's examine some of the results of flirting and compare to how we should represent ourselves as children of God. When a man flirts, he is characterized as a womanizer and only looking for one thing (sex) from a woman. When a woman flirts, she is characterized as promiscuous, disrespected by men and seen as a threat to

---

[52] Romans 8:14 and 2 Corinthians 5:7
[53] Genesis 3
[54] Romans 8:7-8
[55] Galatians 5:16
[56] 1 Corinthians 2:16

women. The flirtatious woman finds it difficult to build friendship with other women so they gravitate to men who take their flirting as a sign of sexual attraction. Flirtatiousness in women will often result in multiple sexual partners that are simply booty calls. Even worse, flirtatious women leave themselves vulnerable to rape because their flirtatious ways are seen as "asking for it" by men who lack self-control. I am not giving the men who rape women a pass because the woman flirted. I taught my daughter not to lead a man on if she did not want to be with him; I taught her that flirting can put her in a vulnerable position.

Outside the Body of Christ, many will reject this teaching because they love to flirt. They will say that I am trying to prevent a natural human reaction. I say that it is not my job to judge but to say what God says. In His Word, God tells us to not be led by our emotions. Outside of the Body of Christ, people will never understand the things of God because the things of God are spiritual and only the Spirit of the Lord can reveal them to us.[57] The Bible tells us that the Word of God is foolishness to people outside of the Body.

But those of us that are in the Body of Christ, we are the ones who have the Spirit of God teaching us and, therefore, our lives and our actions should line up with the Word of God at all times and in everything. The world may believe flirting is okay, but the Word teaches us to be pleasing to God and not man.[58] When we flirt, we do not operate with the mind of Christ. The Bible says that whatever we do must be done to the glory of God.[59] As believers we *court* for our potential husband and wives. When we as believers engage the opposite sex for more than a platonic friendship it should always be to look for marriage and not to just to date around. I will be discussing this more in chapter 5.

Flirting does not bring God glory; it only produces lustful thoughts and behaviors in people. Flirting is a type of temptation and as Believers,

---

[57] 1 Corinthians 2:13-16
[58] Galatians 1:10 and 1 Thessalonians 2:14
[59] 1 Corinthians 10:31

we should never tempt others to sin.[60] Quite simply, flirting is a lie, a deception and the Bible refers to Satan as the Father of lies.

Most of us have lived our lives ignorant of the effects of flirting. With the information and scriptures shared in this chapter, I encourage you to examine your life and ask the Holy Spirit to reveal to you how flirting has led you away from Him. Flirting can be hard to break. I struggled with flirting but I have also learned to take one day at a time and one step at a time. Each day wake with a focus on what God has called you to do for that day and let "tomorrow worry about itself."[61] Pray and ask God to forgive you of your flirtatiousness and to lead you in a life that only reflects Christ. I know you can do it because I am overcoming my battle with flirting and God is no respecter of persons.[62] The Word of God also says that you can do all things through Christ Jesus.[63]

A kiss can turn from being innocent to lustful.

Kissing is mentioned throughout the Bible from Genesis to 1 Peter. I believe kissing was created by God to give us a way to outwardly display love for one another and for families to greet one other.[64] Kissing shows respect, friendship or is used as a greeting; kissing is found in many and various cultures throughout the world. In the Middle East, as well as parts of Europe and South America, people kiss to greet or to show affection. This type of kissing is not a sin because it shows love and respect. In the Bible, David kissed his good friend Jonathan as a sign of brotherly love and commitment. In 1 Peter 5:14, we are told to "[G]reet one another with a kiss of love."[65] If kissing is done to express the God kind of love that we are told in scripture to have for one another, it is not sin.

However, kissing can be wrong if done with the wrong motives. For example, kissing with the intent to arouse sexual desire (outside of marriage)

---

[60] Matthew 18:7
[61] Matthew 6:34
[62] Acts 10:34 (KJV)
[63] Philippians 4:13
[64] Genesis 27:22-26 and 1 Kings 19:20
[65] 1 Peter 5:14

is sinful kissing. Similarly, kissing another to deceive, to gain favor or to betray is also sinful kissing.

At some time in your life, you probably have had a boyfriend or girlfriend relationship. Think back on how a date with your boyfriend or girlfriend could turn from an innocent night out to being overtaken in lust. When on a date, kissing can easily and quickly lead to lustful thoughts of sexual desire; a supposedly innocent kiss can motivate sexual desires for another no matter how saved we say we are. In my backslidden days, I have been on dates with some of the most Holy Ghost filled, respectable and upright women you will ever find in the Body of Christ. However, the date would turn from innocent to lustful in an instant when I would get them in a sensual kiss. While on these dates, I might take the women to the movies and maybe out to eat and everything would be wholesome and godly. But, there would come a time during the date that I would want to get a kiss from the beautiful woman and our innocent date would turn from holy to un-holy. Many times the kiss was not intended to arouse sexual desire or "turn the woman on," as we say; but, the kiss would invariably ignite something between us and I was not about to turn that desire off or turn the sex down. Fornication was often the result of what started out as a harmless kiss. You may be thinking, "How holy could these women be if they would so easily get in bed with you?" But, the Bible tells us to "take heed lest" you fall.[66] In the Bible, some of our greatest men and women of God had weak moments (e.g., Adam & Eve, Abraham, David and Peter). If you are honest with yourself in examining your kissing experiences, you will agree that there is rarely, if ever, anything harmless about kissing when done with the thought of arousing sexual desire.

Kissing done to deceive or to gain advantage is a sin. In movies, we regularly observe how both men and women will use a kiss to flirt with a boss, co-worker, teacher or someone with authority. In these instances of flirting, the kiss is designed to win the person over to a point of view, to entice or control. Using a kiss in this manner is un-Godly, wrong in every sense of the word and should be avoided. Even if you think that there is no

---

[66] 1 Corinthians 10:12 (KJV)

other way to convince the person to see your point of view or to give in to your requests, do not use kissing to entice or gain advantage over another. Many people use kissing to better their own lives and they leave the people they've tricked dazed and confused. Kissing for these purposes is deception; the person kissed believes the other person has feelings for them. In fact, the point of the kiss is to deceive and to make the person kissed believe that the person kissing cares about them. Once the favor is given or the request granted, the person kissed is abandoned and left feeling lonely, heartbroken, stressed and angry.

The Bible also talks about the kiss of betrayal; Judas gave Jesus a kiss right before he went out to betray Him.[67] I have never seen anyone betray another with a kiss like Judas did Jesus, but we can learn a lesson from Judas' actions. Kissing to deceive or to take advantage is often done to entice another to sexual intercourse whereby the sex is used as a way to gain control or advantage. A deceptive kiss is also used to entice to fornication with the intent to show others that the person enticed has poor character and cannot be trusted because they gave in to the temptation. In no way is it Godly character to betray another's trust, love and kindness. The Bible tells us to love one another as we love ourselves.[68]

When kissing is acted upon with ungodly intentions it can be devastating.

Kissing done with the right motives and intentions can be a gesture of submission to another, of love and of friendship; it is viewed by God as a lovely act and encouraged throughout the Bible. However, when kissing is acted upon with ungodly intentions, it can be devastating to the parties involved. Let us make sure our kissing is godly so that we do not fall to the temptations of this world. Jesus taught us to be watchful at all times so that we don't fall into temptation, because the spirit is willing but the flesh is weak.[69]

---

[67] Matthew 26:48 and Mark 14:44
[68] Luke 10:27
[69] Matthew 26:41

CHAPTER FIVE

In the Game: Dating and Relationships

Do not be yoked together with unbelievers …
What does a believer have in common with an unbeliever?
(2 Corinthians 6:14-15)

In the Bible, marriage is the only relationship between a man and a woman that God recognizes and blesses. Dating, however, is not mentioned in the Bible; so *I* don't teach dating. It is an activity that has developed through our culture and I believe that most of what takes place in dating defeats how God wants His children to live.

In my opinion, I believe the best pattern and course of action for believers is courting. Let me explain the difference between the two. In our culture, dating is considered a modern form of courting but is really something very different. Historically, courting is a man meeting and getting to (platonically) know a woman with the intent to marry that woman. In the past, courting never took place without the specific intent to marry. Courting sometimes took place after an arranged betrothal (agreement to marry) and even after marriage because it was specifically designed for the man to win the affections of the woman he had intentions on marrying or had married. Dating has become a part of our culture in the last 100 years, since the early 20th century. Dating as we know it today is a recent phenomenon.

We were never intended to follow the world's system or way of doing things. Paul wrote in Romans: *"Do not conform any longer to the pattern of this world, but be transformed by the renewing of your mind. Then you will be able to test and approve what God's will is--his good, pleasing and perfect will."*[70]

---

[70] Romans 12:2

What we typically think of as dating is when a man and woman publicly "go out" with one another. When dating, you "go out" with whom you want, you go where you want, when you want, to do what you want, and for whatever reason you want. Modern dating is done to have fun or "hang out". Many times those dating want Mr. or Mrs. Right-Now, in other words "I just want someone to hold me for a while." God wants us to have a good time but within the confines of His Will. Jesus said, *"I have come that they might have life, and have it to the full."*[71] Dating can lead to marriage but is often messier than courting and will bring unnecessary baggage into the marriage relationship that could have been avoided.

When courting, you are following the Holy Spirit.

There are levels and stages in courting and I will touch on a few of them here. Courting is done so that a man and a woman can get to know one another when there is an interest to marry. When courting, you seek and follow the leading of the Holy Spirit. Therefore, courting is always done within God's will.

Before I go further, let me say that you should never focus on getting a spouse. Your focus should always be on the Kingdom of God so that you are in the right position to be blessed with a mate. The Bible says: *"But seek first his kingdom and his righteousness, and all these things will be given to you as well."*[72] There are too many women and men doing nothing other than waiting for a husband or wife. That is NOT how you get a mate. Just as in the story of Ruth, the Lord <u>and</u> your Boaz should find you being faithful to what God has assigned you to. Do all things as unto the Lord, for God releases a spouse to you when you are diligent and faithful in the work He has assigned you to.

When I met my wife, she was in the church serving water to the pastors and ministers. Before I ever approached her, I observed her faithfully tithe; every other Sunday she was in the Tithe Line. I observed her faithfulness to other things as well, like assisting the drama department

---

[71] John 10:10
[72] Matthew 6:33

build sets and hang costumes for the plays. I also observed her sincerely and longingly praise and worship God. I saw her physical beauty but what most attracted me to her was her faithfulness to the things of God. Without making it obvious, I asked around the church about her and discovered that no one could get to her; I was told she was uppity. In Christian circles, when a person is called uppity, it often means that they know who they are in Christ and will not settle for just anyone approaching them. This was the case here. Even though I was backslidden at that time, deep down inside I knew who I was and knew the call on my life; this was a woman that could go with me into my future in God.

This testimony about meeting my wife exemplifies what is the first step in courting: observation. Webster defines observation as gathering information by noting facts or occurrences. Don't allow yourself to get the reputation as the man or woman who has been through the whole church, that is, one who has been involved with or had relationship with many in search for a mate. STOP SEARCHING for anything other than God. If you become attracted to or are interested in another, observe their actions and habits first; observing the person of interest will help you to be more selective about to whom you give your time. The habit of observing will require focus and you will be more watchful in your life endeavors.[73] Observation will also require that you know who you are in Christ and to have direction in Christ; you must first know where you are going and what to look for.

I would not have you ignorant; the man finds a wife and not the other way around. The world teaches that the woman can find her a man and that the Bible is culturally antiquated for our lives today. The Word of God says: *"He who finds a wife finds what is good and receives favor from the LORD."*[74] If you take the Bible to be truth, we can move on.

In Proverbs 18:22, the "find" means to discern. When a man determines a woman is wife material, he has found a good thing and can

---

[73] Matthew 26:41
[74] Proverbs 18:22

then approach her as the Holy Spirit leads him in courting her. Anytime you see the word "good" in the Bible it means beneficial. For example, when God made light in Genesis 1, He saw "it was good." In other words, it would benefit those for whom He created the light. If you are a man who has decided to observe a woman to get to know more about her, you should do so with a focus on whether she will be a benefit to what God has assigned you to do for the Kingdom. As mentioned previously, this type of observation would require you to first know your assignment in life before you start looking for a wife. That is why the Word says to "seek first his kingdom and his righteousness"; everything in your life should benefit what God has ordained for you to do for the Kingdom. Women, once a man approaches you to court you, you should then observe him to determine that he, in fact, is husband material.

You may ask how you would observe another (man or woman). If you attend the same church ministry, that should be easy. Observe the person's faithfulness to the things of God. If you do not attend the same church ministry, organize group outings where you can assess character, personality, likes and dislikes. Additionally, observe the person's communication. The person's communication should give you a good idea of whether you are compatible and would be equally yoked with that person. Equally yoked simply means you both have an equal understanding of the things of God. Without stirring up too much, ask common friends about the person you are considering. Try also to observe the person in different public and social settings; people change in certain settings, good and bad.

After a time of observation, the next steps in courting are the approach and intention stage. This is when the man approaches the women to say "I feel we should look into courting; these are my intentions and this is what I have to offer." Men, be aware that the woman you approach may say she is not ready and that she needs to pray about it or she may give you a straight "No." Don't be discouraged. My wife told me "No" a couple times. Some men may be led to speak to their Pastor, mentor or a wise friend before approaching the intended. Some women may be led to speak to wise counsel as well before responding. I recommend keeping the number of people with whom you discuss your observation to a bare minimum.

If the woman agrees, move next into the courting stage. I believe courting should always be done in groups; leave as little opportunity as possible for the devil to come into the relationship. I say court in group settings because if you are alone with someone of the opposite sex, you are vulnerable to becoming intimate with them, e.g., kissing and hugging and more. If you are intimate during courting, your judgment will be clouded; soul ties are real and they are strong.

There are a few things that should take place during the actual courting stage. While you engage in group outings together, gather information about each other's family, including medical history and strongholds in the family. The two of you should agree on guidelines such as "we will never be alone" so that you can get to know one another unhindered by the consequences of intimacy outside of marriage. Setting these guidelines will help to preserve the integrity of the courtship so that you can honestly assess such things as whether or not you have similar interests.

During courting, discuss with one another what you believe you are to accomplish in Christ, how many children you would like to have, whether or not either of you have been married before, where are your parents in all this and the things you have observed about one another that you don't like. When you talk about the things that you have observed that you don't like, honestly assess whether or not you could live with that character or personality trait for the rest of your life. If you enter into a marriage covenant with this person, that character or flaw comes with the covenant. The list goes on and on as to what to discuss and observe about one another during courting.

Make sure you take the time to go through these initial stages of observation, intention and courting. However, once you decide to marry, you should begin Christian Marriage Counseling. At this stage, you can bring in children from a previous relationship; start to do things together with the children. I have more about children in the next chapter: Courting with Kids.

During the courting stage, if you decide not to marry this person, stop courting; there is no need to spend any more time with someone whom you do not intend to marry. In all of this, be prayerful and follow the Spirit of God.

When a relationship is ordained by God you will complement one another and add to one another.

We should always be in relationships that benefit us. Many begin relationships with unbelievers because they don't understand their value. When you don't know your value you will make decisions that will diminish your worth. If you don't realize that you are precious gold then you might sell yourself off as silver or brass or even copper. Most of the people we choose are beneath us if we don't recognize our value; we downgrade. However, if we know our value we will seek to upgrade. Anything that is not real for our reality will be considered counterfeit and rejected when we know our worth. More specifically you need to know what God has called you to do, what he purposed for your life, and your assets; so you will make a wise decision in choosing a mate.

You should pray for a spouse, but it should not be for your focus. In other words pray the Lords will for your life and allow the Holy Ghost to lead you through God's will. In the church, there is so much focus on getting a husband and a wife, that many miss developing the Kingdom agenda. When your focus is on getting a spouse, the enemy can easily trick you. The enemy will use that against you and can corrupt your flow, but if you seek the kingdom first everything will come into place. If you are interested in a person that is not interested in you, it could be because God is protecting you from where that other individual may lead you - they can stop the progress and altar your destiny.

There are many woman and men that do not come to add to your life but to leech from your life, I call them succubus. Notice everything in the Bible says add to your faith this, and so on and so forth. God is all about addition and multiplication (the only time he take away is when he separates the wheat from the tare). Deceptive people will come into your life with nothing to offer. I believe that God wants everything to benefit, he calls it fruit. But there are facsimiles of men and women that come with no helpmeet, no direction and no vision. If they come with nothing and you have something, know they are coming to take from you. Some want to simply be a girlfriend or boyfriend; others just want to be the 'other' woman or man. These are mindsets that just want to have a 'right-now' relationship; I don't believe any of these relationships are in line with God's will for us.

If a man comes into your life with no vision – he is going to wastefully use up the resources that God gave you, which were meant to attach to a vision that a man of God should have. Ladies, your time, mind, talent, and even your drawing power (whether through beauty, body or personality) will be used up. God uses your resources to get you to your destiny, a destiny that was intended to build for the Kingdom. I believe men should be looking for *favor* on a woman which results in fruit in her life. She has the very drawing power of God, which will be used in your marriage to complete the vision you were given from God. This favor is shown in the book of Ruth. She was found gleaning in fields and favored by Boaz. Gleaning is operating in opportunity and seizing the moment. A woman who is favored brings increase from her opportunity. When a relationship is ordained by God you will complement one another and add to one another.

CHAPTER SIX

Kid and Play: Courting With Kids

"But if anyone causes one of these little ones who believe in me to sin, it would be better for him to have a large millstone hung around his neck and to be drowned in the depths of the sea."
(Matthew 18:6)

Sometimes children have to be considered in courting because they have been born to the man or the woman out of wedlock or are living with a divorced parent. It's sad but it happens.

If you are interested in marrying a woman, her children and your children will always be a factor at each stage of courting. A popular radio show host and comedian has released a relationship book telling women to allow children to interact with the person right away so they will know if the relationship should continue. I disagree. Sometimes a parent poisons the mind of the child to destroy anything the courting parent could possibly have with a good person. The child is not the one running things.

I believe children should be introduced only during the courting stage. You can't base your relationships on what the child feels. The child is not developed enough in the things of God or in life experience to give much assistance in the observation stage. My daughter was about twelve years old when she met my wife, Nicole. Based on preconceived notions that they had about one another, neither one cared much for the other. Nicole never had a real father in the picture and did not understand why I spoiled my daughter. As time went by, Nicole understood things better and my child understood things better. If I had based my observations and my decision to court Nicole and my daughter, Sacha's feelings, for one another, Nicole would not be my wife today. There will be times you will have to deal with the immaturity of the other parent of your child when you are courting with children involved.

It's important to find out as much as you can about the other person before you bring that person around your children. You should have a lot of questions asked and answered before children are ever introduced in the courting stage. If you attend the same church ministry as the person you want to court, monitor how that person interacts with their own children (if they have children). Is the person a good mother or a good father? Is the person protective of their children? How does the person interact with other people's children or the friends of their children? Watch for a perverted spirit or a sprit that does not care for children. Upon careful watch, you can pick up on anything that might be a red flag in the person's interactions with children. For example, if that person has children and never talks about their children, that's a red flag! If the person never mentions responsibilities that they have to take care of with their children, that also is a red flag! RUN!

If you have fly-by-night relationships, it hurts your children.

Once children are introduced in courting, plan events together with the children to help break the ice and help the children transition in their interactions with this new person in their life. Make it clear to the person you are courting and to the children that they all are important in your life and you love them all. Also, make it clear that neither is going anywhere. The person you are courting and the children have to work it out. Once again, be clear that children should only be introduced in courting when you are seriously headed toward marriage. Children need stability; fly-by-night relationships hurt the children.

There are times when children are still hurting because their parents are no longer together. It is unfair to the children to bring people in and out of their life; they might get attached. Doing this causes more damage than waiting until you both are seriously headed toward marriage. In a situation where children interact with a person who is in your life and around them all the time (what I call "counterfeit marriage"), the child will start to place that person as a parent figure. When the person is no longer in the life of the child because the two of you have broken up, the child grows with a twisted image of a parent. Furthermore, the child will view God in the same twisted way they view parental relationships: they will see God as unfaithful and not to be trusted. God says He will never leave you or forsake you and will be with you until the ends of the earth;[75] anything other than faithfulness is not a part of God's character.

Some years ago, I counseled a woman in her late thirties who had three children from a prior relationship. This woman came to me because she was stressed about helping her boyfriend of two years. He had been there for her and her children in every way since their relationship began. Three months prior to our meeting, he lost his well-paying job in the construction field. Now he was struggling financially and having difficulty finding employment. She felt obligated to help the boyfriend because of all he had done for her and her children. I explained to her that it was incorrect for him to be in that position in her life and them not be married; she should have been trusting God to take care of her. She was not supposed to be receiving help from a man who pretended to be something he wasn't; he was, in fact, not her husband or the children's father because they were not married. This man may have good intentions but he was not in line with the Word of God. Because he was in the wrong position in her life, she was feeling obligated to continue in a wrong relationship with him. Some of you may think this is harsh but it is truth.

If a friend has an emergency and you need to extend a loan, that is okay; but neither of you should be paying the other's bills. To pay another's bills is to enter into an agreement with that person. Women who look to men to pay their bills are in the wrong position in that instance. If you are entering into friendships with men to get your bills paid, you are operating with wrong motives. Essentially, such a woman is flirting and pretending to want a relationship with the man when all she wants is what the man can provide. There are women that are engaged in relationships with men because they have mouths to feed; that is not a Godly relationship. That person's heart is deceptive. God looks upon the heart. Women should not engage in such deception and men should not allow a woman to put them in a position of head of a household when the two are not married!

---

[75] Hebrews 3:5

CHAPTER SEVEN

The Low-Down: Homosexuality, Bestiality and Everything In Between

"Furthermore, since they did not think it worthwhile to retain the knowledge of God, he gave them over to a depraved mind, to do what ought not to be done."
(Romans 1:28)

Homosexuality and Lesbianism are hot topics in the 21st century. Many people are fighting hard on both sides of the battle to prove that they are correct in their understanding of how God made us to express ourselves sexually with one another. Popular culture today promotes the belief that men and women have the right to marry whomever they please whether they choose a homosexual or heterosexual relationship.

Over the years, American opinion has changed dramatically on this topic. In a 1987 survey on homosexuality, 75% of Americans believed that homosexuality was wrong; but in a 2010 survey on the same topic, only 44% believed homosexuality to be wrong. It is considered the norm today to believe that people can have sex with whomever they want and however they chose. The belief that sexual conduct should have nothing hindering freedom of expression has become so popular that it has attached itself to the civil rights movement in the USA; it is considered a civil and personal right of liberty to be allowed to be as sexually perverted as the mind could conceive. Many who are outside of the church and even inside the church believe that the sexual preference of a person is their private choice and is right before God if they love the other person. The issue has turned from being about sexual preference to being about the right to love another.

However, what does God have to say about homosexual relationships? The Bible clearly tells us throughout the Old Testament and in the New Testament that Homosexuality and Lesbianism are wrong. Here are some scriptures to ponder and meditate:

- Leviticus 18:22
- Leviticus 20:13
- Romans 1:26-27
- Jude 7

There are many more scriptural examples throughout the Bible that show us God is not at all pleased with homosexual practices. However, instead of just quoting scriptures and just telling you that the practice of homosexuality is wrong, I would like to take a practical look at why God tells us not to engage in homosexual relationships.

God's Original Design

Many advocates of homosexuality say that some are naturally born to sexually desire a person of the same gender. These proponents of homosexuality believe that it is about the flow of life and that homosexual expression should not be suppressed or prevented. This belief suggests that our Creator made us this way, that God intended for a man to desire another man sexually and for a woman to desire another woman sexually. However, this belief contradicts the Word of God.

The Bible says that God made man and woman in his own image and likeness.[76] The man and woman were to be sexually active with each other only. Their sexual organs complement each other and it was God's original design and purpose that they only be with each other. Now, if God had made man to be with a man and woman to be with a woman we would have seen God say it in the book of Genesis. Many believe God does allow homosexual acts but if this is true, why would He say afterwards that homosexuality was wrong? This would be contradicting the image and likeness he made us out of if we were created with a "natural" desire to be with the same sex. He would be condemning us for something He gave us and that would make Him a hypocrite and an unfit to be God. So, the thought that God made homosexuals that way is wrong and it does not have any Biblical bases. God man Adam and Eve perfect in every right, they were

---

[76] Genesis 1:26

49

the physical representation of God on the earth. They walked, talked, and aced like God and there was no sin in them until they decided to go against God's word. God did not create them with any kind of sinful nature so the thought that people are created by God already designed to sexually desire the same sex is wrong and misleading.

We should not confuse the sinful natural that Adam and Eve brought into the world with God's original design. I believe that people are born with different sins to which they are inclined; these proclivities often come from generational bondage in a family. In my counseling experience with homosexual individuals, very often a family member had struggled with the stronghold of homosexuality, like a grandfather, father, mother, uncle or aunt. Often the person had been molested or raped by someone in their family who was of the same sex. Whichever the case may be, it shows that God did not make some men or some women to be homosexual; it is our sinful nature that causes us to sin against God. I also remember growing up and noticing that some young boys were more friendly with other boys than the rest of us. If we agree with popular belief, these boys were created by God to be attracted to boys rather than attracted to girls.

God's original design for us included procreation. Homosexual couples cannot achieve the God-given mandate to man to "... *be fruitful and multiply.*"[77] God is a God of purpose and nothing He does is ever wasteful. If He intended for a man to be with a man, He would have provided a way for the two men to "... *be fruitful and multiply.*"[78]

As was discussed in Chapter One, two men or two women cannot procreate. Since that is the case, God was wasting His time and earthly resources in designing someone to be homosexual. It is contradictory to God's nature to be wasteful or not to have purpose for all that He has created. The sexual organs of a man and woman are designed specifically for the opposite sex.

---

[77] Genesis 1:28
[78] Genesis 1:28

God is love.

Homosexuals claim that the desire to be with a same-sex partner stems from the love they feel for that person. Even some of the Churches today believe that homosexuality is not a sin because of love. They say that God's command to love one another supersedes everything else. To further support homosexuality, they continue by saying that the scriptures in the Old Testament of the Bible do not apply to the New Testament church and that there is no commandment against homosexuality in the New Testament. Furthermore, they conclude that people are free to be with whomever they want as long as they love them the way Christ teaches us to do. This false teaching has become popular in some Churches today but it does not stand true to the Word of God. Romans 1:26-27 speaks directly against homosexuality and Jude 7 reflects on God's anger toward Sodom and Gomorrah for the debauchery and sexual perversion practiced by the inhabitants of those two cities, including homosexuality. These false teachings are designed to justify homosexuality or to stay politically correct within society.

No matter the motive for the false teachings about homosexuality, this is a good time to define what love is so that we will understand what love is not. The Merriam-Webster dictionary defines love as a profoundly tender, passionate affection for another person. In 1 Corinthians 13, God defines love: *"Love is patient, love is kind. It does not envy, it does not boast, it is not proud. It does not dishonor others, it is not self-seeking, it is not easily angered, it keeps no record of wrongs. Love does not delight in evil but rejoices with the truth. It always protects, always trusts, always hopes, always perseveres."*[79] Continuing in the Word, 1 John 4 says: *"Whoever does not love does not know God, because God is love."*[80] The latter part of that verse sums it all up: "God is Love."[81] If God is love, then you have to have a relationship with God to have love. When you have a relationship with God, you have a relationship with His Word because God and His Word are one.[82] If God is Love and He and His

---

[79] 1 Corinthians 13:4-7
[80] 1 John 4:8
[81] *Id.*
[82] John 1:1

Word are one, then anything that contradicts the Word of God is the very opposite of love. What the world calls love is not love; love is never outside of God's will.

Homosexual practices are against God's Will for mankind; homosexual desire does not stem from love but from lust. Lust is love perverted; lust is what we enter into when we are operating outside of God's Will for our lives. Lust is a stronghold from the enemy that manipulates the love of God in us and has us thinking that our fleshly desires are love. Our fleshly desires are not love; God is love.

Satan has led us to believe we are actually fulfilling God's will in our sin.

Our relationships with others are critical to success in life because we were made to bless one another and build one another up. God also commands us to love one another. When lust is mistaken for love, the bond is hard to break. Operating in lust, Satan has us believe that, in our sin, we are fulfilling God's will. In reality, when we operate in lust we are abusing ourselves and abusing the other person whom we say we love.

In homosexual relationships, the spiritual oneness that a married couple is to experience under God is counterfeited. When two people come together sexually, they are not coming together just in the flesh but also in the spiritual realm. When a man and woman seal their covenant of marriage in sexual union, God blesses that spiritual union and the marriage is sealed by the Holy Spirit. When this spiritual connection happens outside of God's plan, the connection is bonded and sealed by Satan; we give Satan control in that relationship. Giving Satan control of our relationship allows him free reign to steal from us, to kill and destroy us.[83]

As Kingdom Citizens, we should stand on the Word of God as our truth even if we are going against popular culture. God's truth is that homosexual practices are wrong no matter how much people say they love one another or feel they were made to be with the same sex. When God calls it wrong, it is wrong. We will experience in our lives the consequences of

---

[83] John 10:10

our bad relationships; the Word of God clearly tells us that what we sow we will reap.[84]

You do not have to act on or act out the thoughts Satan puts in your mind.

Another aspect of this homosexual discussion is that men claim to be gay because homosexual thoughts come to mind. The enemy regularly and consistently bombards your mind with un-Godly thoughts; the (spiritual) battlefield is the mind.[85] The Bible says that all sin is common to man,[86] which means that every single person has the potential to commit every kind of sin. It is only the Grace of God that keeps us from committing sin. Thoughts placed in your mind that are un-Godly and unholy are more often than not a trick of the enemy; if he can get you to dwell on homosexual thoughts, he can convince you that you are a homosexual. The Bible tells us in Proverbs that whatever we think about we shall become.[87] Satan will use curiosity, confusion and the media to make you open and susceptible to his schemes to destroy your life. If you consider, ponder and dwell on the unholy thoughts placed in your mind by Satan, you will eventually act on those thoughts.

When God created mankind, He divided the responsibility to care for earth into two parts – male and female.

Effeminacy describes a human male who exhibits traits usually associated with feminine nature, behavior, mannerisms or style. The effeminate spirit comes from our sinful nature; this spirit attacks men at the very core of who they are in God. Because God is a God of purpose, everything He does has a specific purpose in His Kingdom and He has a goal for that purpose. When God created mankind, He divided the responsibility to care for the earth into two parts: male and female. The Male and the female are, together, co-rulers of the earth; each has specific responsibilities as they operate in the dominion power that came from God

---

[84] Galatians 6:7-8
[85] Romans 12:2
[86] 1 Corinthians 10:13
[87] Proverbs 23:7

at creation.[88] With this in mind, the tactic of your adversary, the devil, is to always corrupt the plans of God so that God's plans and purposes for life on earth will be thwarted and fail. We see the first instance of how the devil operates in his actions toward Eve in the Garden of Eden; Satan distorted God's Word to Eve about the tree of the knowledge of good and evil.

The effeminate spirit diverts (steals) the male-man away from the purpose for which God originally created him. If the devil is successful in diverting the male-man, then his position is left void and humanity falls; both male and female responsibilities need to be accomplished and fulfilled for successful life on earth. God gave us the mandate to operate in dominion power on the earth; if we are to live a successful life on earth, we must maintain fellowship with God's Will. When a man tries to be a woman or a woman a man, they leave a void in that purpose for which God designed them male and female; the result is abuse of themselves and of the people around them.

For example when a son looks to his father to be an example of what a man should be, he will get a distorted view of what is male and what is female when he can't tell his father from his mother. The homosexual example that is being set before this son will conflict with the man inside of him and cause problems for him in his future. I have actually seen this happen to a man.

The other situation is when a male child is raised by lesbians. Even when the women don't teach the young man to act like a girl, it is common for the young boy-man to take on womanly traits. This occurs because the young boy-man is seeing both male and female roles acted out in front of him by women. This is also an example of the importance for men in our society to act like men and not little boys! They need to stand up to their responsibilities and be the fathers to their sons that God has called them to be. Sons are getting the wrong understanding of the male role in our society because of the lack of real, Godly men operating in their lives. A young man-child should not learn to be a man from watching TV, movies or from

---

[88] Genesis 1:26

what he heard in a song; he should get his understanding of the male role from the Word of God.

In chapters 1 and 2 of Genesis, God made Adam and gave him his assignment to be the male-man of the earth; He first called Adam to remain always in His presence and placed Adam in Eden. In Hebrew, the word Eden means, "a place or an atmosphere." God placed Adam in the place of His presence and also called Adam to cultivate the garden. To cultivate means to make something better than its original state, that is, to make everything in his environment better than its original state: his wife, his family, his job, his school, his church and his friends. Men are called to make everything around them better.

God also called Adam to be a teacher; he was responsible for teaching Eve the Word of God. God gave Adam His Word about eating from every tree except from the tree of the knowledge of good and evil. He also told Adam how he was to name the animals and to rule the earth. Adam taught Eve everything God had told him. In the home, men are the teachers of the Word of God. But a man is not capable of teaching the Word if he does not know God's Word for himself. So, all you men who think that going to church is for women, you are supposed to be leading and teaching the women about the things of God and not the other way around.

As a man, Adam was supposed to protect the garden. Men are called to protect their families with everything they have; this is why men are built with more muscles than women. The muscles are designed to help the man to protect his family from harm. Therefore, a male-man is called to provide for his family, spiritually, financially, physically and emotionally. The male-man is the source from which the family pulls what it needs. If you are a woman reading this book and you have a son who does not have a father in his life, keep a close eye on your son. Speak what God says a man should be to your son so that the Holy Spirit can bring back to his remembrance what God called him to be as a male-man. In addition, look for other men at your local church who might mentor your son and show him a good example of what God called a man to be.

The effeminate spirit is dangerous to mankind and is part of the plan for the enemy to kill us.

Can you see why it is important for a male-man to be who God called him to be? When he does not fulfill his purpose, he puts unnecessary pressure on the woman. The woman is designed to help the male-man rule the earth not to rule it without him! This is why so many women today are going through depression and emotional distress because the male-man is not taking his proper place on the earth and society is crumbling right before our eyes. The effeminate spirit is dangerous to mankind and is part of the plan for the enemy to kill us.

Transgender or transsexual behavior is a by–product of the effeminate spirit.[89] The effeminate spirit is a direct attempt by Satan to destroy God's plan for humanity. When a man tries to be a woman (and a woman tries to be a man), the two will never be able to fulfill the opposite gender's God-given purpose. It doesn't matter how well either may look like the opposite sex or if they get a doctor to perform surgery so they could have the sexual organ associated with the gender they want to be in life, they cannot fulfill that gender's purpose. Why? Because they are still male or female on the inside. Just because we choose to follow our own plans in life and choose not to follow God's plans or we change or pervert God's plans, God's plans are still in effect; to be happy, successful and fulfilled in this life is for a man to fulfill his role as a man and for a woman to fulfill her role as a woman. When you live as a transgender, transsexual or transvestite, you are living in bondage.; anytime we live contrary to God's Word we are living in bondage. When people who are transgender, transsexual and transvestite are led into homosexuality, a stronger bondage develops because of the spiritual ties that take place during sexual intercourse. Satan uses our lustful desires to get us to abort God's plans for our lives. Transgender, transsexual and transvestite

---

[89] Transgender and transsexual behavior specifically relate to a person, male or female, who does not conform to or think of themselves in the way that is considered normal behavior and gender-role for their sex. Some people confuse transgender and transsexual behavior with the transvestite fetish. Although the transvestite will exhibit transgender and transsexual behavior, the transvestite fetish specifically speaks to a fetish to do what we call cross-dressing, that is dress differently than your natural gender-role would call for.

behavior is mankind's attempt to abort the purpose of God for life which will only lead to heart break and sorrow.

Bestiality is sex with an animal.

Bestiality is not as popular in our culture as premarital sex but it does take place throughout the world, even in the USA. Bestiality is when a person has sex with an animal. You may think bestiality is a new phenomenon; however, in Leviticus 18 God had to give the children of Israel a commandment not to practice bestiality.[90] God called bestiality a sin back then and it is still a sin today.

Bestiality is unnatural on many levels. One reason bestiality is unnatural is because different species cannot procreate; human beings cannot procreate with animals the same way that cows cannot procreate with pigs. They are different species; God created species to only procreate with their own species!

In Genesis 2, the Bible says that none of the animals were suitable for Adam.[91] Bestiality denies the God-given hierarchy of mankind over animals. God created mankind in His own image; not the animals. Animals are not able to distinguish good from evil nor are they able to reason or to rule the earth. For mankind to have sexual relations with an animal would be to lower himself/herself to the place of an animal which is not where God called humans to be. God told mankind to "... *rule over the fish of the sea and the birds of the air, over the livestock, over all the earth, and over all the creatures that move along the ground.*"[92] God told us to have dominion over the animals not to be one with them.

Pain has never been a form of pleasure given by God.

Another sexual perversion is the use of whips, chains and confining body suits during sexual intercourse. Popular culture believes that this masochistic sexual interaction is needed to spice up the sex life of a

---

[90] Leviticus 18:23
[91] Genesis 2:20
[92] *Supra*

57

couple. Stores and online shopping sites provide a variety of options for people to practice masochism. There is even a name for this form of sexual interaction: sadomasochism, meaning deriving sexual gratification from pain. Sadomasochism is predicated upon pain and fear, which is exactly the opposite of what God wants us to experience in life and especially in the bedroom. Sadomasochism is predicated on one partner dominating the other to the point of the dominated partner allowing the domineering partner to inflict pain. Allowing your partner to inflict pain on your body is a sign of that partner's complete dominance over you. God never told us to have dominion over another human being; He told us that we were supposed to dominate the earth and the animals.[93]

Sadomasochism is against our very nature and goes against what God designed for sexual interaction. Pain has never been a form of pleasure ordained by God nor has He ever told us to inflict pain on another or ourselves for the pleasure of it. Sex is supposed to be an expression of our love, selflessness and affection for one another. To inflict physical pain or verbal abuse is NOT PART of God's plan for the bedroom. When a person gets sexual release from hurting others or from getting abused themselves, they have succumbed to the works of the enemy. The enemy is always trying to get us to inflict pain on ourselves because He hates everything that God has blessed.

We must also remember that as children of God our bodies are the temple of the Holy Spirit. [94] We are to honor our bodies in everything we do, whether that means being careful about what we eat and drink or being careful about what we put our bodies through. This includes what we put our bodies through in the bedroom. One way to think about it is to ask yourself if you would go to a church and throw a rock through the window or go inside and vandalize the place. Most of us would never even consider doing this to a church building or any other religious facility. If that is the case, then why do we take our bodies so lightly, which is the Temple of the

---

[93] Supra
[94] 1 Corinthians 6:19-20

58

Holy Spirit? We won't tear down a religious sanctuary but we are willing to ruin our bodies with all types of activities, such as smoking, drinking, eating fatty foods and allowing others to abuse our bodies during sexual intercourse.

God wants us to enjoy sex; sex is designed to be pleasurable and exciting in the marriage bed. Even though the world and, sometimes, the church, paint the marriage bed as boring and routine, that is not how God ordained it to be. If you read through God's book of marital love, the Songs of Solomon, you will find that the marriage bed should be a fun and entertaining experience for married couples. The foreplay of kissing, touching and licking is a part of the pleasure God wants us to have. The problem is that many of us experience lustful sex years before we marry and the lust environment is controlled by the enemy, not God. So, we have sowed the wrong sexual experiences into our lives and into our bodies. God's will can be brought into our marriage bed, but we will never experience God-ordained sexual pleasure outside of His Will. As I discussed earlier, we will hurt our marriage relationships if we try to transform what we did in lustful relationships to the marriage bed.

I can testify to this in my marriage. I had been having sex for many years prior to my marriage and enjoyed many aspects of BDSM (Bondage, Discipline, Sadism, Masochism).[95] It had gotten so deep into my spirit that it was extremely hard to break and when I tried to approach my wife with it she was turned off and it caused a riff in our marriage. I was hurt because I didn't see the demonic influence it had on me. I felt like I had more fun living in sin than living right before the Lord. This is a tough place to be in when you look at your life and it feels like life was more interesting and exciting before you got saved. It feels like living saved is boring and it causes many to question whether it is even worth it. For this reason, many Christians fail in their marriages because they are trying to relive their lustful sex life prior to marriage; this is impossible to do. When you try to

---

[95] "BDSM represents a continuum of practices and expressions, both erotic and non-erotic, involving restraint, sensory stimulation, role-playing, and a variety of interpersonal dynamics. Interest in BDSM can range from one-time experimentation to a lifestyle, and there is debate over whether a BDSM or kink sexual identity also constitutes a form of sexual orientation." (Wikipedia, 2013. Retrieved from http://en.wikipedia.org/wiki/BDSM.)

do this, you set your marriage up for failure. I have counseled many people who come to me and say, "my husband doesn't do it right" or "my wife is boring because she doesn't like me to choke her." These are people who, like me, were trapped in the demonic bondage of lustful sexual desires. BDSM brings a spirit into the marriage that will affect other areas of the marriage as well; the BDSM spirit will even affect the children.

We must be careful not to abuse our bodies because our bodies are the Temple of the Holy Spirit. Jesus Christ was our example of how to live for God on earth and he never did anything to hurt Himself or anyone else. On the contrary, Jesus healed people of bodily pain. We need to follow Him in this and bring love and healing, not pain and hurt, to our spouses and to our marriage beds.

CHAPTER EIGHT

Can't Stop: Sex Addiction, Nudity and Body Worship

"Therefore God gave them over in the sinful desires of their hearts to sexual impurity for the degrading of their bodies with one another."
(Romans 1:24)

It is a common belief that men have stronger sex drives then women. In most respects, this is true except for women who are oppressed with nymphomania. Nymphomania is defined as "excessive sexual desire in a woman."[96] A nymphomaniac is most commonly believed to be a woman who is insatiable in her sexual appetite; she is seen as a woman who goes from man to man trying to satiate what she believes is sexual desire. However, the search for sexual satisfaction is a false search because what the woman really desires cannot be fulfilled in lustful sexual encounters with men. The search in which these women engage creates a vicious cycle that tears up their bodies, their families and their careers.

Nymphomania derives from the spirit of lust; women are not born nymphomaniacs. Nymphomania develops over time. Some women are prone to nymphomania because of strongholds passed down through the family lineage; but any woman who opens herself up to a man in lust leaves the door open for the enemy to attach the stronghold of nymphomania to her life. Many women oppressed with nymphomania are found to be prostitutes because they have learned that they can make money in their addiction to sex. But, women who engage in numerous sexual relationships are fragments of who they really are; each time they take a man into their body in sexual intercourse, they lose a piece of themselves in the process.

Prostitutes are not the only women who suffer from the sexual addiction of nymphomania. Nymphomaniacs can be found in our churches, teaching our kids in schools, driving the buses on which we commute or

---

[96] Merriam-Webster Dictionary (online), 2013. Retrieved from http://www.merriam-webster.com/dictionary/nymphomania

working in jails and running businesses around the world. Many women suffer from the spiritual bondage of nymphomania; we are unaware of the magnitude of this sexual addiction. Nymphomania goes unnoticed because women are better at hiding their secrets than men. Nymphomania can manifest in excessive behavior; many nymphomaniacs are not looking for fulfillment in the area of sex but looking to be fulfilled in other areas of life, which could be physical, emotional, spiritual or psychological. In my experience, the spiritual bondage of nymphomania is due to an unfulfilled spiritual longing, so the women, instead, please their flesh. The void that the nymphomaniac is trying to fill can only be filled by the Spirit of God.

The woman is a helper to the man and co-ruler with the man.

Nymphomania attacks women because they are a help-meet and co-ruler on the earth with man. When a woman subjects herself to being abused by men through sex, she is stepping out of line with her authority and leaving her God given assignment unaccounted for. The nymphomaniac is taking from more men then she was designed to handle. God wants a woman to be married to one man. When a woman is sleeping with many men, she is becoming one with each and every one of these men and bringing many demonic spirits upon her and her family. A woman is designed to be a helper to one man but when she is with many men she helps no one. Thus, the woman is left spiritually unfulfilled because she has many men in her but she can't do anything for any of them except give herself sexually. The woman sinks into depression, and is tormented and broken because she is not positioned in her rightful place. The spiritual frustration from which the woman suffers leads her to the bed of another man and the cycle continues. Satan plays with her thoughts and convinces the woman that sexual gratification is what she seeks; but this is far from the truth.

All forms of spiritual bondage were brought into the world because of the fall of Adam and Eve in the garden. As we humans became exposed to spirits other than the Spirit of God, it became hard to do the right thing. The Apostle Paul talks about this in Romans when he said "*I do not understand what I do. For what I want to do I do not do, but what I hate I do. …. As it is, it is no longer I myself who do it, but it is sin living in me." [97]*

Many women do not realize that sexual addiction stems from the sin that is living inside of them. Women (and men) will often think that sexual addiction is because they are out of control without realizing it is a sin like any other. Sexual sins are no greater than any other sin but harder to break because they are sins against the body.[98] Sexual sin allows soul ties to take place between two people. A soul tie is when two spirits become one flesh or are knit together; the Bible says this happens when two people come together sexually. The term soul tie is not found in the Bible but is commonly used to describe the connection that is made in the spiritual realm when two people come together in sexual intercourse. Soul ties bring unholy connections between two people that cause destructive behavior.

I have counseled women who stay in abusive relationships because they are one with a man in the spirit and can't seem to get away in the physical. It seems so obvious to people looking in from the outside that the woman needs to get away from the dangerous relationship but she just can't seem to break away. She feels like she is still in love with him or that she needs to help him become a better person. This is an example of how the enemy takes a woman's God given responsibilities to be a helper to a man and use it against her when she is operating outside of the will of God. If this kind of tie occurs with a woman who is dealing with just one man, what do you think women who are nymphomaniacs are going through since they are dealing with more than one man?! Soul ties open the door for people to be manipulated by others; women are controlled by the men they are sleeping with and the only ones benefiting are the men. I have seen women get into a life of crime and violence because of a soul tie with the wrong guy. These were girls from good families and with a solid church background and financial stability; nevertheless, these women turn from everything they were taught and raised in to chase after a boy. These women usually end up throwing their lives away, end up in jail or, worse, dead. It's sad to see but it

---

[97] Romans 7:15
[98] 1 Corinthians 6:18

is the truth of the matter. Women who battle sexual addiction are most often subject to emotional, verbal and psychological abuse. They are preyed on by men and kept in psychological slavery that leaves them depleted and desolate.

Nymphomaniacs are also prone to homosexuality. As explained above, the nymphomaniac will never find in fleshly pursuits what she is really looking for. However, the lack of sexual satisfaction from men leaves the woman open to alternative options to try to find sexual satisfaction. I have witnessed women go from man to man to willingly being gang raped at orgies and then turning to another woman to find sexual satisfaction. They try everything possible to fill the void and every time they have sex with someone the problem gets worst. The sexually addicted woman believes she is trying to get satisfied but she is actually strengthening the bondage; sin is progressive.[99]

The sexual addiction that leads to multiple sexual partners in a search to fill a spiritual void is not just found in women but also in men. The term nymphomaniac describes a woman but there are men also who are oppressed by excessive sexual desires. If a man continues to have sex outside of the will of God, that is, outside of marriage, he opens himself up to the stronghold of excessive sexual desire just like the nymphomaniac. In my life, I have battled with excessive sexual desire that is the same as the nymphomaniac experiences. Every woman with whom I slept made me want another and another. I was so caught up that I was sleeping with as many as 5 to 6 different women a day; most of the time it was not 5 to 6 at one time but there were times I had multiple sexual partners simultaneously. My mind was on sex when I was at work or spending time with my daughter at the park or while in church; my mind was on sex all the time. Even in church as a Pastor, SEX was on my mind. Many Pastors won't admit their struggles but I believe we help our congregations more when we are honest with them about our addictions and struggles. As a Pastor, I find that when I open up and let others know the issues with which I have

---

[99] Romans 1:28

struggled, it makes it easier for them to reveal their struggles to me so that I can minister to them.

"You, dear children, are from God and have overcome them, because the one who is in you is greater than the one who is in the world."[100] As strong as is the bondage of being a nymphomaniac, stronger still is the Blood of Jesus Christ. Only God can deliver a woman (or man) from sexual addictions and He wishes that you, dear man or woman, would walk in deliverance from sexual addictions. The apostle Paul tells us that when we are born again we are a new creation and *"old things are passed away."*[101] These old things to which Paul refers are not just the sins and habits we had before we were saved but every sin and all of the sinful nature that Adam and Eve brought upon us in the fall. If you are a born again believer, any sinful nature that tries to take hold of you has no legal right to do so. If you are not born again, there is nothing you can do to totally break away from the enemy because the Blood of Jesus has not yet set you free because you have not accepted His sacrifice on the cross. The benefit of being a Kingdom Citizen is that Satan can do nothing to totally hold you down. You have the right to walk in victory unless you chose otherwise. Believers who are trapped in sin are doing so willingly and cannot blame anyone but themselves.

Advertisers use models to subliminally suggest a standard image for everyone.

Looks are everything in America! In the USA, models are glorified and advertisers use models to deliver the subliminal message that body image and appearance can deliver happiness. The consequences of subliminal messages are that we have 90-pound 15-year-old girls starving themselves because they think they are too fat; the image of beauty they see in magazines and on TV appears thinner than their own 90-pound body and they want to be happy so they try to conform to those images. Similarly, guys go to the gym 3 to 4 times a day to try and gain muscle on top of muscle. They take steroids to improve their looks and to conform to a

---

[100] 1 John 4:4
[101] 2 Corinthians 5:17

certain body image, which later on leads to major health problems and sometimes death. Women take 2 to 3 hours to get dressed just to go grocery shopping and will pamper themselves for hours upon hours for the sake of looking good. People should always look their best when they are in public and there is nothing wrong with putting your best foot forward. However, there is such a thing as becoming a body worshipper in our attempts to look good.

Body worship is when we jeopardize our health, our finances and our families for the sake of personal good looks. It is also more than the personal satisfaction of looking good, but an excessive desire that translates into actions to conform to a cultural standard for body image and appearance. These image standards are perpetuated through magazines, the Internet and over the TV. Body worship is when you care more about how you look than who you are. To go even deeper, you define yourself by how you look. People who body worship may wake up with bags under their eyes or gain a little weight or spill something on their outfit and they flip out; they may become angry and irritable with the world because their appearance is flawed. They also are constantly looking in the mirror and asking others for compliments on their looks so that they can have a sense of security. If a body worshipper is dissatisfied with what they are wearing or how they look, they are emotionally crushed or become angry and sometimes even violent. Living in America, it is easy to understand how this addiction to looks can occur. However, let's take a few minutes to examine what are God's standards for image and appearance.

Jesus is the greatest teacher there ever was and He gives us insight into how we should approach image and appearance. In Matt 6:25-34, Jesus brings deliverance to born again believers: He tells us to not worry about what we are going to eat, drink and wear (appearance). He explains that worrying will not solve our problem(s) and, therefore, we should just not worry. The good news is that we have a Father in Heaven that will take care of things for us.[102] The word Father in the Greek is "Abba," which means "source" and "sustainer." Jesus reveals to us that God is the source in which

---

[102] Matthew 6:32

we will find all of life's needs. God is also our Creator and is the one who sustains us throughout every test and trial of life! This is exciting news for a believer because our Father tells us not to concern ourselves with what the rest of the world does.

Most importantly, Jesus tells us to focus on the Kingdom of God and His righteousness (staying rightly in line with the Kingdom).[103] During this passage of scripture, Jesus says not to focus on what we will wear or on our appearance.[104] I believe He shed light on this point because during that time period and even today people are overly occupied with their looks. People were so occupied with appearance that it turned into body worship. It doesn't seem like things have changed much! I have seen people in the church today who may not serve another god, but they worship their own bodies. They are their own god and they serve this god with time, talent and treasure. The Word of God tells us not to have another god before Him.[105] God wants us to focus less on outward appearance and more on the inward person; what is inside, in the heart, is what is most important to God. He reveals this to us in 1 Samuel 16 when He is talking to the prophet Samuel about picking a new king for the children of Israel.[106] He tells Samuel that He does not operate like men; He does not look at the outward appearance but at the heart. The children of Israel had a king they had chosen, which was Saul. They chose Saul based on how he looked on the outside; they saw how tall he was and that he looked like a king and they picked him based on his outward appearance. Saul turned out to be the wrong choice. God also desires that we keep our bodies under subjection[107] and that we not give our bodies over to sexual immorality, alcohol, smoking, excessive weight gain or unhealthy weight loss; even our ego should be kept in check.

Worshipping our bodies and the bodies of those around us is a trap of the enemy to take our focus away from the things of God. Society wants us to give our time to outward appearances but God wants us to give our time

---

[103] Matthew 6:33
[104] Matthew 6:28-29
[105] Deuteronomy 5:7
[106] 1 Samuel 16:7
[107] 1 Corinthians 9:27

to inward appearances, which pleases Him. As Kingdom Citizens, let us want to please God more than man (or our flesh). Remember the lesson of our King in Matthew, Chapter 6, and leave the worries of life to our (Abba) father who is our source and life sustainer. Put your attention on the Kingdom of God and stay in right alignment with God.

We are not to look at other people in their nudity.

Many people love to be naked; they enjoy displaying their nude bodies so that others can see. In the world, there are nude beaches, nude colonies and, of course, strip clubs. The infatuation with nudity drives many of the world's economies today. On TV and in the movies, we are bombarded with nude bodies or scantily clad actors and actresses. When people are criticized for watching nude bodies, some may say that Adam and Eve were naked in the Garden; they call it natural and don't see any reason to cover up.

What does the Word of God reveal to us about nudity? In the book of Genesis, God created Adam and Eve and they were placed in a garden called Eden. We know that Adam and Eve were naked in the Garden because it was not until they disobeyed God (Chapter 3) that they realized they were both naked.[108] Why did it matter to Adam and Eve all of a sudden that they did not have covering for their bodies? From the beginning of their existence, they had seen each other naked but now they were ashamed of that nakedness.

To get a clear understanding of what happened, we must first recognize that what took place was in the spiritual realm first and then in the natural, physical realm. Before Adam and Eve sinned, they were in the Garden of Eden which was God's very presence. Because Adam and Eve lived in God's presence in the Garden of Eden, they were always and eternally covered spiritually and physically with God's Glory; there was no need for a physical covering just like God did not have a physical covering for His Glory. In the Garden of Eden, God's Glory was able to flow

---

[108] Genesis 3:7

undisturbed between heaven and earth. I believe Adam would watch how God ran things in heaven and, then, he would duplicate on earth what he saw done in heaven.

When Adam and Eve sinned, God's presence had to leave the earth because God is a holy God and He cannot be in the presence of sin. Adam's and Eve's eyes were opened to their nakedness;[109] they were disconnected from God first in the spiritual realm and then in the physical realm. Because of sin, Adam and Eve were now open to demonic influence because they had lost their covering and were no longer in God's presence as they were before. Adam and Eve now needed covering for their earthly (physical) bodies. This is why God came looking for them (He already knew where they were). God had compassion on Adam and Eve and came looking for them to give them animal skin to cover their earthly (physical) bodies.[110] I believe that the animal God killed represented Christ in that Christ would be the sacrifice to once again cover man from his nakedness.

Throughout the Bible it tells us to cover ourselves and not to become nude in any type of public setting. It also tells us that we are not to look at other people in their nudity. Here are some scriptures:

"And thou shalt make them linen breeches to cover their nakedness; from the loins even unto the thighs they shall reach."[111]

"Ham, the father of Canaan, saw that his father was naked and went outside and told his brothers. Then Shem and Japheth took a robe, held it over their shoulders, and backed into the tent to cover their father. As they did this, they looked the other way so they would not see him naked."[112]

A person's nudity is a representation of the fallen state of mankind. God requires us to keep ourselves covered except with our marriage partner with whom we are one under God's covering. Every other form of nudity is not acceptable to God. We have to keep this in mind when we watch TV

---

[109] *Id.*
[110] Genesis 3:21
[111] Exodus 28:42
[112] Genesis 9:22-23

and movies. Many people succumb to the lust of the eyes because, as a culture, we spend billions of dollars each year on strip clubs, pornography and magazines that display nudity. We must keep in mind what Jesus told us in Matthew 5: *"But I tell you that anyone who looks at a woman lustfully has already committed adultery with her in his heart."*[113] Jesus is clear in this scripture that when we look at a woman (or man) who is naked, we allow ourselves to be overtaken by lust which leads to other strongholds.

As Children of God, we must stay in line with what God tells us to do even when our flesh may not like it. Through the power of the Holy Spirit, we are able to defeat the urges to be publically naked; that same power is available to deliver us from every kind of lustful habit or action. God can and will deliver us from any and every bondage in which we find ourselves if we will just let him do it by His Spirit.

---

[113] Matthew 5:28

CHAPTER NINE

The Waiting List: Sex Education for Your Children

"Only be careful, and watch yourselves closely so that you do not forget the things your eyes have seen or let them slip from your heart as long as you live. Teach them to your children and to their children after them."
(Deuteronomy 4:9)

We are living in a time when parents must be diligent to teach children about sex. We cannot be evasive when we have those discussions but must be candid and open to our children. It is imperative that our children get the right information from God's point of view; they will surely be exposed to the wrong information in the world and we want God's Word to have already been planted in their spirits.

Being open about sex and sex related topics can be accomplished without using graphic images or explicit language. For instance, when my son was six years old, he saw his younger niece come out of the restroom. He was in shock because she did not look like him. I clearly and openly shared with him that he had a penis and she had a vagina; he was male and she was female. When he continued with questions of curiosity asking what was the difference (between girls and boys, men and women), I explained: "Well, the penis is made to give life and the vagina is made to receive life and multiply." I put it in plain words and explained that the female body was made to become pregnant from the sperm that came from the penis and to hold the developing baby in the womb. I also expressed that diseases can be transmitted during sex.

If we don't give this basic information to our children, they will become curious and explore on their own; they will, invariably, fall prey to the consequences of their ignorance, which often leads to teen pregnancy and sexually transmitted infections. The enemy wants you to believe that openly sharing sex-related information with your children will make them want to explore all the more. But that simply is not true.

The Bible says *"My people are destroyed from lack of knowledge."*[114] The destruction mentioned in this scripture includes children. When something is destroyed, it means that it has been cut off or its life force ceases. When we fail to share the truth about sex from God's point of view with our children, we are cutting them off to the abundant life the Lord promises in His Word.

I am a gun owner, so I taught my son to shoot a gun at a young age. I showed him how the gun works and the damage it can do. My son is less inquisitive about guns than he was prior to learning about them with me. He received his information in a safe environment and from a trusted source. Without a shadow of a doubt, he knows that the gun will kill if he pulls the trigger.

Children need this information to protect themselves.

By the time children begin nursery school, they are already curious about sex. When I was in the first grade, I would give a little girl in my class pretzels every day so that she would lift her dress up for me to see her vagina. No one ever said anything to me about what was under her dress; I was just curious about what she had. Many will say that children in nursery school are too young to know about that; "they are innocent," they say. However, the truth is that we are all born in sin and shaped in iniquity.[115] Children may be innocent in the fact that they have never had sex but they are capable of, and do think outside of the will of God; this is the basis of the sin nature. Romans 3:23 says: *"all sin and fall short of the glory of God."* In this scripture, "all" means the whole human race, and children are included. We have to train our children to operate in the Spirit of the Word at a young age, which gives them the weapons they need to defeat the sexual perversion Satan uses to destroy them.

Children need this information to stay protected. Child molestation and child rape are rampant in our society; children need to know the distinct difference between good touch and bad touch. Children need also to know

---

[114] Hosea 4:6
[115] Psalms 51:5

they can come talk to you freely. Even young ladies and teens need to know that sex is made strictly for marriage and that sex outside of marriage is wrong. Anyone trying to get you to have sex with them outside of marriage is trying to lure you out of God's perfect will for your life.

Boys start to touch themselves as early as 3- and 4-years-old. As I shared with you earlier, I was led into sexual perversion at an early age and trapped by an addiction to masturbation for over three decades. No one ever said anything to me about it being wrong or right. I was locked in a sex-prison that eventually affected my marriage. Tell children that they are going to want to touch themselves because it feels good but that we were never meant to stimulate ourselves. Tell children that we were meant to be sexually stimulated only in marriage by our husband or wife. Tell your child or teen that masturbation is not of God and it will put them in a bind. With the information that you give them, they can struggle to fight those urges rather than give in to them and think that it is normal to give in to the urges. The information you give will result in fewer struggles with sexual addictions in their life.

The number one spirit that comes against children is perversion. Molestation will have a little girl thinking that her purpose is to orally stimulate a man or woman or to be subservient sexually. A girl with this mindset is messed up for life. If a little boy experiences anal sex with a man as his first sexual experience, he will battle in that area most of his life even if he is not a homosexual. When he marries, he will probably have homosexual fantasies during sexual intercourse because it has become part of his sexual experience. Very often, men who are molested as a child marry but still cannot climax unless they imagine a man performing anal sex or by engaging in anal sex with their wife. Either way, it is bondage; the enemy desires to get our children while they are young.

Look with me at a conversation that Jesus had with Peter in Luke 22. Jesus said: *"Simon, Simon, Satan has asked to have all of you, to sift you like wheat. But I have pleaded in prayer for you, Simon, that your faith should not fail. So when you have repented and turned to me again, strengthen and build up your brothers."*[116] The original text utilizes the Greek word exaiteomai, which, in this context, means to ask that one be given up to one from the power of another. Now, it's silly that Satan would ask God to give up one of His own; but what Satan is really asking is "let me prove that all of them are not really yours. If I tempt them, I will show that they will deny you and I will prove they won't live upright before you." When Satan asks God to let him sift Peter as wheat, he was referring to a process to remove the chaff, which represents the worthless and evil portion of the wheat. If Satan can pervert our children at a young age through masturbation, rape, voyeurism, lustful conversations and pornography, etc. he can corrupt their thinking and frame who they become.

Don't leave much alone time for your children or give others access to your kids.

Molesters are always going to be in the world. We protect our children by giving them information about what signs to look for. We also protect our children by limiting those who would have access to them on a regular basis. As parents, we should be very selective about who can watch over our children in our absence; the list of child-sitters should be very, very small. I am disgusted by all the mothers who will leave their children in just about anyone's care. Your children should be in your care mainly but when they have to be absent from you for any reason, you should have an already scrutinized list of very few people. Otherwise, your children could be exposed to spirits that would give the devil access to kill, steal and destroy in your child's life. You may not need to be concerned with the person monitoring your child but concerned with whom they allow in *their* presence and in *their* homes. Statistics on child abuse indicate that children are often molested by people they know or when they are in a familiar environment, like at a friend's house or with a child care provider. When children are molested, they are being set up for messy personal relationships and dysfunctional marriages.

In our society, we believe in teaching children not to go off by themselves or with strangers. In addition to that, we should teach our

---

[116] Luke 22:31-32

children to pray and we should pray regularly with them. Since we cannot be with our children 24/7, the best protection we can give them is knowledge and understanding of God and who God is and how important it is to have a relationship with God. As it says, we should raise our children in the way they should go; teach them how to live a pure life.[117]

Even though I teach my child to live right, I also teach him about things like how to use condoms so he is not ignorant of Satan's devices and knows how to use them (just like I taught him about guns). I will not give my child a condom because he has to live by the rules of my house; however I do give him information about how to use a condom in case Satan lures him into a trap. For example, I don't bungy jump because it is taking an awful risk with life; but if you are going to go bungy jumping, make sure all the harnesses are in place and everything secure. We must give our children the information that will create good knowledge to help them recognize when they are doing risky things. Teach your children about AIDS and STDs/STIs. I discuss these more in detail in Chapter Ten.

Similarly, I don't believe in giving birth control to children, but I do believe in teaching children about pregnancy, birth control and condoms. Make the information available but don't give the birth control to them; giving it to them is like giving your permission to use it and they should not be having sex. Explain to your daughters that sex will hurt the first time because the hymen is broken; explain the purpose of the hymen related to the blood covenant of marriage. Don't scare them with stories of your own pain; let them know the pain will soon turn to pleasure and an addiction could take place if they are not doing things God's way.

Children should not be left unsupervised for long periods of time.

Don't leave much alone time and access to your children. I know a story of a little girl who's mother worked many hours and, therefore, she was often home alone. One day, with sex being far from her mind, she let a friend of hers come over; he was a slightly older boy who forced himself on

---

[117] Proverbs 22:6

her. This sexual experience caused the young lady to have a distorted mindset about men and she ended up in a horrible relationship years later. Children must be guarded and covered.

Threatening to kick your child out if they have sex is not effective. The way is to give them the information, pray and ask the Holy Spirit to help them. When you talk with them about sex and sex-related topics, you should have a healthy attitude; be candid but don't cause your children to be fearful about sex. I believe we should be talking to kids about these things at the ages of 6- and 7-years-old because at 8- and 9-years-old, many children are already having sex or they have friends who are having sex. I recently counseled a young lady who said at 8-years-old, a 12-year-old boy forced her to perform oral sex on him. No telling how long he had been doing this. When your child is informed and has knowledge about some sexual matters, they are more likely to make good decisions.

Do not be unequally yoked with un-Believers; always think of your future when making decisions.

Train children not to be unequally yoked and what that means; children have to be trained who to choose as friends. The world will tell them that friends are anyone with whom they associate but that is far from the truth. The dictionary online describes a friend as someone with whom we have a "bond of mutual affection."[118] Teach children that it takes time to develop a bond and they should not give a new acquaintance access to their life or to their time. Explain that being in the wrong place at the wrong time with the wrong person could cost them their life. Help your child to think of the future and not just the here-and-now.

Getting to know someone and making as more than a friend takes time.

There are many teens and preteens that want to date and or have boyfriend/girlfriend relationships, but as I stated before I believe in courting. I believe its best to only go on group outings; no one-on-one time together. The flesh is weak; take it seriously. Teach children that when they

---

[118] Google Search (2013). Definition of "friends."

are around someone they like that they should not be alone with that person. Explain that feelings for that person will develop as they spend time and get to know the person, and that they may even have constant thoughts about the person. I don't believe children should have a boyfriend or a girlfriend; their relationships with one another should just be as friends. Explain to your daughters that a guy will say a girl is his girlfriend so that she doesn't talk to another guy. If we are taught correctly as children, we will grow with the right mind set about friendships, courting and marriage, which will vastly improve our relationship experiences.

Our culture is so entrenched in the boyfriend and girlfriend relationship that it has eased its way into the Kingdom of God; this should not be so! We are not of this world; we are in the world but not of this world.[119] We are Kingdom citizens if we are saved; Kingdom rules of engagement are different than those of the world.[120] We must repent, that is, change our way of thinking and come in line with God's Word. We have to renew our minds; read and study the Word of God to rip out those old thoughts and ways and replace them with God's thoughts and ways. The world denies God as creator and, instead, explains creation in terms of "evolution." If the world is so wrong about something as basic as creation then why are we taking its advice on relationships?!! We should not be following the world's rules; God has already set rules by which we should live. We have God's Word and that's what we should stand on at all times.

Parents should teach children the Word of God at a young age.

From the ages of 1- and 2-years-old, there are scriptures you should be reading to your children. For example, Ephesians 6:1: *"Children, obey your parents in the Lord, for this is right. Honor your father and mother--which is the first commandment with a promise--that it may go well with you and that you may enjoy long life on the earth."* Psalms 34:11: *"Come, my children, listen to me; I will teach you the fear of the LORD."*

---

[119] John 15:19
[120] John 16:33

Fathers are the priests of the home and should be leading and guiding the children as they grow. If there is no father in the home, the mother needs to be priest; this means that mothers should be making sure that everyone in the home is fed spiritually as well as physically. You priests (Father first and then Mother) are responsible that all who are in your home is serving God; if anyone does not want to follow God then they can't stay.

We are all capable of committing any sin that any other person on earth could also commit.

I would be saddened if my child came to me and said that he believes he is homosexual. However, this is a situation that would need to be handled very carefully. I would show him the Word of God where it says that all sin is common to man.[121] In other words, the same sin that you would do is the same sin that I or a neighbor could also do. As part of our sin nature, we all could potentially commit the sin of homosexuality because we are all born in sin and shaped in wickedness. I would explain to my child that we all fall short of the glory of God and that we all could have homosexual thoughts. We can all have homosexual feelings as well, but we do not have to act on our thoughts and feelings. I would show him in the Word that God's design for a man is to only be with his wife, someone born a woman. We have to teach our children that God can change those desires and thoughts and feelings. We will be in for a battle, but God's Word can and will deliver. In everything, let your children know that they are loved by you and by God.

Watch and pray and try the spirit by the Spirit.

If there is an effeminate spirit or even a suicidal spirit on your child, it doesn't matter. Your relentless and persistent trust (faith) in God's ability to deliver and in the integrity of God's Word will overcome anything the child is going through. God watches over his Word to make sure it accomplishes what it should accomplish, and to confirm that it makes its way prosperous![122] Your faith in God's Word will produce the Grace needed for your child. We

---

[121] 1 Corinthians 10:13
[122] Isaiah 55:11

are to keep our children in an atmosphere of Holiness and under the anointing so that any foul spirit will have to leave. Walk before your children as a real man or real woman and they will begin to emulate what you are exhibiting. Be a real man role model before your children and they will want to be a real man and follow your example. If your son walks around with his wrist bent and he sees a real man does not have his wrist bent, he'll start to straighten that wrist out. Test the spirit by the Spirit and be watchful of the spirits that might come around your children; scrutinize the people that are in your home and around your children. Do you really want a person with an effeminate spirit around your children? That spirit will affect your child and the person will set the wrong example before your children.

I explained to my son that a man does not drag his feet; he began to observe who drags their feet. One day he asked: "Dad, why do women drag their feet? Why do those men that act like girls drag their feet?" I said to him, again, that a man does not drag his feet; "the devil wants that man to think he is a woman, so he drags his feet." If you explain things to children, they will start to observe and compare what they observe with what you have explained to them. If I had not talked to my son and given him the information he needed, he would not have known that real men do not drag their feet. Now he knows a man picks up his feet when he walks.

The wrong spirits can get to our children while they are in the womb if we leave the door open for Satan. The door to the womb can be open to Satan if we engage in things like illicit sex, abuse of prescription drugs or the use of recreational drugs (marijuana, ecstasy, etc.); the mother hanging out in ungodly environments will also expose the unborn fetus to wrong spirits. There are many strategies that Satan uses to get at our children, like molestation, neglect or child abuse; he will use anything and everything to take our children off course. If our children are to have a chance for the abundant life that Christ died to bring us, we must fight for our children through prayer, living a Holy lifestyle before them and faith in the Word of God. It is an injustice to the child when he or she is raised in a household not serving God. If you are clubbing or doing drugs change your lifestyle so it does not affect your children and family. Also, closely monitor what the children in your home are watching on TV; the TV and the music videos on TV are the most likely place for the child to get wrong information about how to live life!! God is holding us accountable for the protection of our children.

CHAPTER TEN

The Three-Letter Word: HIV, AIDS and Stds

" If my people, who are called by my name, will humble themselves and pray and seek my face and turn from their wicked ways, then will I hear from heaven and will forgive their sin and will heal their land. "
(2 Chronicles 7:14-15)

We find people infected with STD's and STI's in urban neighborhoods as well as suburban neighborhoods; none are exempt and no one is safe from the potential of catching one of these infections. Some diseases and infections can be treated and will go away with a properly prescribed medication. However, medicines will only mask symptoms in other infections and the victims are left with re-occurring flare-ups or scars that are a constant reminder of the lack of wisdom and of the mistakes made in younger days. Guilt, hurt, pain and defeat rule in the lives of millions of people throughout the world because of STD's and STI's. Some have committed suicide; still others have taken their pain out on loved ones because of the heartache and shame that they live with from being infected with an STD.

As of 2013, over 7 Billion people on the earth; approximately 315 million of those live in the USA. It is estimated that 1 out of 5 in America have an STD/STI, 80% of whom do not know they have been infected because symptoms do not show up right away. People are spreading STDs/STIs to others before they realize that they have, themselves, been infected; unfortunately, this becomes a revolving cycle for many.

God put a plan in place for our sex lives and we should have a clear understanding of God's purpose in that. As we can see from earlier chapters, God's plan is for sex to only take place in marriage. As it relates to the discussion of STDs and STIs, living life God's way will, potentially, save our lives and protect us from destroying our health.

In the book of Genesis, we find the story of the fall of man and how sin brought judgment to the earth because of the fall of Adam and Eve. Every disease on earth is part of that judgment, including the common cold, HIV/AIDS and cancer; ultimately death also came to the earth.[123]

The Bible warns us that sexual sin carries a built-in judgment from God. In 1 Corinthians 6:18, it says: *"Flee from sexual immorality. All other sins a person commits are outside the body, but whoever sins sexually, sins against their own body."* When a person commits a sexual sin, they are doing more than disobeying God; they put their bodies in jeopardy. Our bodies are given to us by God and are the temple of the Holy Spirit if we are children of God. Our bodies were given to us so that we could relate to our environment here in the physical world. We are spirit, body and soul; our bodies allow us to live here on the earth so that we can fulfill our God given purpose. So, when we have sex outside of God's plan, we open up our spirits to Satan; similarly, we also give Satan permission to touch our bodies with the curse of diseases that came to mankind as a result of the fall of man. STD's are dangerous to our purpose in God because they attack our health and make our bodies vulnerable to illness. The results of being infected with an STD or STI will also bring with it the spirit of depression because of the societal guilt, shame and humiliation that the victims endure. Many infected with an STD/STI live isolated because they made a mistake that they cannot fix. STD's/STI's are a direct attack of the enemy to destroy us and to ruin the lives of those around us.

God knew when Adam and Eve sinned that the earth would have to endure things that He never intended for mankind. God gave us laws and statutes to protect us from the pitfalls we would find living on earth in our fallen condition. God told us not to have sex before marriage. If you ask a doctor, scientist or school counselor, this is the best prevention from being infected with an STD or STI. Additionally, cultures that live in strict adherence to God's principles and His plan do not experience the magnitude of STD or STI infections as in the rest of the earth. Sexual freedom turns out not to be so sexually free; it is more akin to sexual bondage! When you are

---

[123] Genesis 3:19 and Romans 5:12

having the illicit sexual intercourse, it may seem to be liberating but the consequences come with devastating effects.

We see the result of living "free" from God's Will in that today teens and young adults are being infected with STD's/STI's at an alarming rate; the enemy is trying to kill off a whole generation! My generation and the generations of my parents and grandparents adhered to more strict observation of God's plan for us; these prior generations did not have such high percentages of youth infected with STD's/STI's. I watch as my granddaughter grows up in a society that says it is okay to do whatever it is you want to do and whatever your mind can conceive. If you want to have sex with another woman it's okay; if you want to sleep with a different man every night, it's your prerogative; if you want a career as a porn star, that's too is okay. We live in a society where prostitution (both men and women prostitutes) is seen as part of the GNI (Gross National Income).

The sexual culture of the USA tells us to fully explore (**and** experience) our sexual desires as a way to know ourselves. The sad part about this climate of free sex is that the discussion of freely exploring sexual pleasures is at opposite ends of the cultural and political spectrums from the discussion of how rampant are STD's/STI's in our society today. If a young girl wants to remain a virgin until marriage, she is ridiculed and sometimes called stuck up. If a young boy wants to remain a virgin until married, he is also ridiculed as not being masculine and even as being gay. Sexual freedom and the fight against STD's/STI's should be a part of the same discussion but rarely is.

When our youth are encouraged to freely explore sexuality, they should be told that the highest chance of catching an STD/STI is if they are a young American especially black females. At the same time that condoms and birth control are being dispensed to youth, they should be told that a life can be tragically altered by one night with the wrong person, no matter what protection they are wearing. It is a trick of the enemy to get us to focus more on the sex (that is, having free sex or the consequences of unprotected sex) than to focus on God's plan and purpose for sex in marriage. Even a discussion of STD's/STI's is not really where God's Will would have us focus.

The fact is that we bring judgment on ourselves in accordance with 1 Corinthians 6:18 when we have sex outside of marriage. The Word of God says we will reap what we sow.[124] If we sow disobedience to God, we will reap death and disease. I am not saying that everyone with a disease sinned against God and that being infected with an STD/STI is their punishment. Some have been infected through non sexual ways, such as a baby being born with HIV because the mother was infected, or a person had innocent contact with another who had HIV/AIDS or the infection was transferred during a blood transfusion. But, the fact of the matter is that we all have been impacted by sin and need to lean on God's forgiveness, grace and mercy to make it during our allotted time here on earth.

---

[124] Galatians 6:7-8

CHAPTER ELEVEN

Sex in All the Wrong Places:
Pre-Marital Sex, Lust, Fornication, Abortion, Virginity and Adultery

"Thou shall not commit adultery."
(Exodus 20:14)

If more people understood the severity of fornication and adultery, I believe few would allow just anyone to come into their bodies. When you receive Jesus Christ, you become one with God. God does not want you bringing random relationships into your union with Him. Bottom-line: your body is not your own.

Abortion is a sin according to the Bible.

Abortion is a hot topic here in the United States. Our country is divided on the topic between two groups; Prochoice and Prolife. In every major city and small town you can find rallies of millions of people with signs advocating for their side. Political leaders use the topic in their campaign runs, religious leaders speak of it when their congregations gather and community advocates give information about the topic so that people are informed about abortion. However, we as Kingdom citizens must know what God says about abortion so that we are not led by societies opinion but by the Word of God.

The Bible clearly conveys that abortion is wrong. Many will argue that the Bible is incorrect. They dispute that it's the woman's right to choose to keep the child or not because it's her right to do what she desires with her body. This thinking is selfish because the life inside of her does not belong to her, it belongs to God. God designed a woman to have a womb to be responsible to carry the child until birth, but God did not give the woman the responsibility to decide whether the child should be born or not.

God is a God of purpose and He created everything with a purpose. Each child conceived was created for purpose. Recently, a minister told me of a story about a young girl who had a conversation with God during a dream. Since the young girl had an opportunity to talk to God, she spoke with Him and asked questions about how He was performing as our God. She asked "how could He allow us to die from diseases when He says He loves us so much?" God said to her, "I did send the people to create those cures but you aborted them all!" We need to let that sink into our spirits for a minute; we are aborting the solutions to our problems! God works through man for the benefit of man. So when we abort our children we are aborting our benefits. We pray to God for answers, but our selfishness prevents us from receiving the answers to our prayers. Do you see how it is so important that we stay in alignment with the Word of God? Many times our decisions in life can impact the world. Read Chapter 3 of Genesis, Adam and Eve's decisions has impacted all of humanity and will continue to do so until the end of time.

The Bible says that God knows and has a purpose for all children before they enter into their mother's womb (Jeremiah 1:5). God has a purpose for the child but He entrusts us with the responsibility to bring the child into the world. When we have an abortion we are stepping out of line of our responsibility and authority and whenever we do this, we impact not only ourselves but the whole world in a negative way. I have counseled many women who have had an abortion and most of them say they wish they never had. Many of them are haunted by the memoires of there lost children and suffer from depression, suicidal thoughts, and physical complications because of the abortions they have had. God does not want us to destroy ourselves, one another or even the unborn.

If you are a woman who has had an abortion, or a man who has encouraged someone to have one, know that God forgives. Some may maliciously attack those who have had abortions but God does not operate like man. God is a God that will forgive you if you are willing to accept His forgiveness. God does not want His people to live a life filled with condemnation and guilt, so if you have participated in an abortion ask God today for forgiveness and healing.

Jesus is Lord over your body.

If you have confessed Jesus as Lord, He is in fact the Lord over your body. 1 Corinthians 6:15-20 states: *"Do you not know that your bodies are members of Christ himself? Shall I then take the members of Christ and unite them with a prostitute? Never! Do you not know that he who unites himself with a prostitute is one with her in body? For it is said, 'The two will become one flesh.' But he who unites himself with the Lord is one with him in spirit. Flee from sexual immorality. All other sins a man commits are outside his body, but he who sins sexually sins against his own body. Do you not know that your body is a temple of the Holy Spirit, who is in you, whom you have received from God? You are not your own; you were bought at a price. Therefore honor God with your body."*

The Bible says not to keep company with fornicators; it says this because you will become a fornicator. Fornicators will keep lustful spirits in the surrounding atmosphere that will cause you to think about sex; the Bible says what you think about you become.[125] After time spent in this environment, you will become desensitized to those spirits and fall in line with fornication.

Adultery is fornication when you are married. In adultery, you are breaking vows you made before God to your husband or wife. Anytime an oath is broken, the relationship weakens and may eventually be destroyed. Adultery gives Satan full access to your marriage.

---

[125] Proverbs 23:7; supra

The main point of God's Word that you need to understand and get in your spirit is that when you commit sexual sin, you sin against your own body; your body is God's temple.[126] You bring demonic spirits into your body when you fornicate; sex is the gateway to a multitude of sins. As the two become one, whatever is spiritually within one is joining with whatever is spiritually within the other. The consequence of fornication is that wrong spirits, mindsets and desires will guide your sexual relationships – even when you do get married. The stronghold of lust must be broken on both lives for the two to be set free from the demonic oppression picked up in fornication. The relationship forged in fornication was a relationship that God did not honor so He was not directing it by His Spirit. It's not just the marriage license that God honors, it's the vow made to one another before Him. As you live with these lust spirits received in fornication, they are in your life to interfere with the real love God wants in your marriage. When you don't make the vow of commitment in marriage, you allow the hand of Satan in your relationship. Death and life are in the tongue; when you make that confession before God to take your spouse, God comes into that. If you don't make a confession to God but commit an act that God ordained to occur after your confession is made before Him, you are giving Satan permission to be the God over that relationship.

The Bible says that if you cannot contain …

I often hear people say that they have asked God to take away their sex drive. I don't know why anyone would want Him to do that! We were never designed to be without our sex drive. We were designed to lose our virginity only to our spouses, which would herald the beginning of sexual exploration (and the maturing of the sex drive). The sex drive was to grow in the anointing of the covenant of marriage. Premarital sex will cause your sex drive to be forged in lust; lustful sex is unfulfilling and does not work at all in marriage.

Some people enjoy having affairs outside marriage because of the fantasies they have played out in their minds. When you have an affair, the

---

[126] 1 Corinthians 6:15-20; supra

encounter with the other person is brief and fleeting; you are not married to that man or woman nor do you see them every day. You don't deal with all their flaws day in and day out. The person with whom you have an affair will always look great when they are allowed to prepare themselves to meet up with you. Affairs are superficial relationships and premarital sex is fleshly love; both are eros love. When you get used to lustful sex, you will be messed up in marriage until you are delivered from lust. Love, not lust, is what is required in marriage.

The Holy Spirit guides you through right doors, yes, even in sex.

Sex becomes a stronghold when lust is sown in the flesh; whatever you sow in the flesh gets rooted and grows. Premarital sex is outside of God's Will so it does not fulfill what God wants to be fulfilled in sex. The Holy Spirit will guide you through right doors; yes, even in sex. The Bible says: "The steps of the godly are directed by the LORD. He delights in every detail of their lives." This is a principle in God's Kingdom that applies everywhere and at all times.

The word lust simply means strong desire for; therefore, lust is not necessarily a bad thing. You could have a strong desire for a bowl of vanilla ice cream. Many have taken the word lust to be synonymous with evil. Lust is evil IF the thing lusted for is placed before God. When your lust is used by the enemy, he is guiding the lust. God is love; when you are following the guidelines of God, He condones and blesses the love-making.

Relationships sown in lust will become a stronghold; it seems like you just can't get out! Lust takes you to the place of stronghold because anything that Satan guides is done to kill, steal and destroy your life. Lust will have you going back to a relationship that you don't enjoy and don't want; lust will have you fantasizing about being with that person and you don't know why. Lustful spirits will even have you fantasizing about being molested. A young lady shared her story with me and told me that she went into a candy store at the age of 9 and was dragged to the back and raped by the owner. Here it is now, thirty years later and she cannot climax unless she pictures this candy store in her mind and fantasizes about being dragged to the back and raped. Lust will be used by the enemy to thwart sexual satisfaction and have you returning, in your mind, to a wrong situation.

However, greater is He who is in you than he that is in the world!! Hallelujah!! If you submit yourself to God's Word, be willing to let go of the lust, He will heal you and move you into the future where you can experience the proper climax with the proper person. Lust drags you back to hurt but love pulls you forward and up and out of things. When a husband and wife come together in God's plan, they are attracted to one another by eros; when they make love, the soul and the spirit meet and they become one.

A virgin (man or woman) can also be oppressed by lustful spirits. If the virgin has engaged in masturbation, has watched pornography or been regularly in lustful environments, they will marry and have problems in sex because the sex is nothing like their fantasy world has been. It is important to guard your mind so that the wrong thoughts do not create strongholds in your life.

CHAPTER TWELVE

Wrapping It Up

"Wisdom is the principal thing; Therefore get wisdom.
And in all your getting, get understanding."
(Proverbs 4:7; NKJV)

Everything in this book was written to uncover the strategies of Satan concerning sex and relationships. Most importantly, this book was written to educate and edify the people of God by the leading of the Holy Spirit. Use wisdom and discernment when applying the information provided herein. For example, if you are living with a person you are not married to or are pregnant and not married, don't just run off and get married because you are feeling convicted. Get your mind in line with the Word of God first before you make life-altering decisions. You may have made mistakes in the past and feel trapped in the decisions you have made; it would be even more devastating to continue making wrong decisions. You may have done things in your marriage that you are ashamed of; however, we serve a God who is a Restorer of the Breech and who is a Deliverer. We serve a God that forgives the sins of those who have received Jesus Christ, Son of the Living God, as their Lord and Savior. Everything has been washed clean by His blood. The Bible says in Ephesians 2:13: *"But now in Christ Jesus you who once were far away have been brought near through the blood of Christ."* 1 John 1:7 says: *"The blood of Jesus, his Son, purifies us from all sin."* The blood of Christ purifies our hearts (spirits) from activities that keep us from worshiping God.

When you make up your mind to change, the Holy Spirit will help you with the rest; He will lead and guide you to all that is true. We were given free will by God. Remember that the most powerful thing you have is your mind. No one can stop you once you have a made up mind to follow the principles of the Kingdom of God. *"If God is for you, then who can be against you?"*[127]? No one can stop you once you have made up your mind to follow

---

[127] Romans 8:31

the Spirit of God? Let's not waste any more time because the Second coming of Christ is drawing nearer and nearer.

Let me pray for you now: **Father God in the name of Jesus, I pray for the man or woman who is reading this book. It is no mistake, Lord that they are reading it, for you ordained it from the beginning of time. You see their struggles, strongholds and their hang-ups. Your word says in Psalms 103 to remember your benefits; forgive all of their sins, and heal all their sicknesses and diseases. Lord, deliver them now, set them free from the bondages and from the habits that keep them in bondage. I pray their faith won't fail when troubles come and their body begins to scream for what it desires. I also pray they will be strengthened with Your glorious power so that they will have all the patience and endurance they need. I pray that You bless them with all spiritual wisdom and knowledge according to Colossians 1:9. I ask You to give them a complete understanding of what You want to do in their lives. I ask that you help them to live in a way that always honors and pleases You and that they get to know You better and better. In faith, I pray protection over their family, their belongings, their spirit, soul and body in Jesus' name. Amen.**

If you have not received Jesus Christ as your Lord and Savior or want to rededicate your life to Him, there is no time like the present time. The Bible tells you that if you believe in your heart and confess with your mouth that Jesus Christ was God and came to the earth, died for your sins on the cross and rose again three days later, you are saved from the penalty of sin. Death will no longer rule over you. Speak to the Lord from your heart and confess that you are a sinner and need Him to save you. Ask the Lord to fill you with the Holy Spirit. Ask Him to also lead you to a church. There you can be baptized in water, which is merely a symbol that you have died to sin and are now born again in Christ. There you can be discipled and learn to live your life for Christ.

If you are a Believer and do not have a church, find one that teaches the unadulterated Word of God. Ask the Holy Spirit to lead you; Your Heavenly Sheppard has assigned each believer a Pastor (earthly Sheppard) that will speak the Word into your life. This is very important. The enemy has deceived many into believing they don't need to worship with the saints; but we do. (Read Hebrews 10:25.) If you have not had discipleship training, go through discipleship. If there is an insurmountable struggle with pornography or masturbation, find someone that will pray in agreement with you; someone that will stand in the gap for you as an intercessor. You do not have to walk this thing out alone. You are welcome to contact us and tell us how this book has blessed you or if you need us to agree with you in prayer.

May the peace of God, which passes all understanding, guard your hearts and your minds in Christ Jesus.
God bless.

www.thewordcentercogic.com

Biography

A husband, father, and grandfather, J.O. Burns, is the founder of Vision 300 Ministries, J.O. Burns Ministries, and the Senior Pastor of The Word Center Church and affiliate ministries worldwide. He is a graduate of O.M. Kelly Bible Institute and the Interdenominational Theological Seminary New York Ext. The motivational speaker, life coach, and pastor is truly dedicated to building the Kingdom of God.

www.ingramcontent.com/pod-product-compliance
Lightning Source LLC
La Vergne TN
LVHW021409080426
835508LV00020B/2527